TESTIMONIALS

This book had me hooked from the start. It's a wonderful compilation from across the globe about the COVID-19 pandemic - a situation which has impacted us all. Although the stories and experiences are personal and separate in their own right, reading this montage together reminds the reader of the innate fact that we have all experienced the same pandemic, trauma and immense change, and ultimately that we are all one community. What also shines throughout the book is Joanna's connections around the world, the vast diversity of people she has met and built relationships with and how one person can bring and thread a whole new community together - in this case, the community of the pandemic writers. I would wholeheartedly recommend this book to everyone around me, as it creates space and opportunity to reflect and process the events of the last two years. Sometimes we need encouragement to connect with others, practise gratitude and focus on the important aspects of our lives. Every writer in this book goes on their own journey to realise these and as a result, guides the reader to do the same. It is a wonderful book of entwined stories which will have you invested from the start and beautifully reflects humanity and how we deal with adversity.'

Caitlin Fradley. Mental Health Practitioner

I have just read Joanna O'Donoghue's Compilation called *Lockdown Stories*. I was so excited to get my copy, I couldn't put it down as it was fascinating to read so many different perspectives from around the world that were from many walks of life. It was so interesting to hear how people felt through lockdown and what they felt about the laws, the government and trying to get on with life during lockdown. *Lockdown Stories* has something we can all relate to with the Covid-19 Pandemic. It is a great way to remember our current lives and not to distant past. Congratulations Joanna on creating such a wonderful well written Compilation.

Albina Porracin. Author, Coach, Teacher, Consultant, Mentor

Lockdown Stories is an interesting global insight into the varied experiences of life in the COVID pandemic. Joanna has successfully shared snippets of personal history from her family and friends worldwide, which we may look back upon and compare with our own lives during this time.
Having lost several friends and family members during the pandemic, it is refreshing to hear how some struggled through and survived, whilst others moved on to new beginnings. There is sadness, joy, hope and even humour in this book, which holds everything together as we emerge from lockdown to an understanding of a new "normal".

Jane Davies. Retired teacher

Lockdown Stories

Reflections on the pandemic from
around the world

Compiled by
Joanna O'Donoghue

Front cover design by James Homes
Back cover design by Olivia Keer

ISBN: 978-1-7391678-0-6 Print

DEDICATION

This book is dedicated to my family and friends who have supported me through this project.

For my grandchildren, Ella, Theo and Caspian.

A special mention also to my first serious boyfriend, Kevin, who always encouraged me to write.

ACKNOWLEDGMENTS

To my dear friend, Maureen, I thank you for all of your unwavering support and proof-reading skills, for cajoling members of your family to contribute and for welcoming me into your home in France to work on the final edit.

To my son-in-law, Adam, who helped to format the book, as this was a first for me.

Thanks also to Michele who gave help and advice on some aspects of IT and to Olivia for advice on marketing.

Thanks to the readers who provided me with feedback and submitted reviews, Caitlin, Mel, Albina, Jane and Sue.

Finally, thank you to all of the people who have contributed chapters to the book, which made it happen.

A special mention to Deborah Fay from Disruptive Publishing and to the *Authorpreneur's Bootcampers* who I have met online. Thank you!

For the front cover design, thanks to James Homes. For the back cover design and Pandemic Poems picture, thanks to Olivia Keer.

Finally, to you, the readers, I hope that you enjoy reading these stories.

TABLE OF CONTENTS

INTRODUCTION

I had the idea for compiling these stories in the middle of the night early in 2022. That's the time when I have most of my ideas and in the morning, I will have forgotten them. This idea stayed with me, partly because I wanted to record my own experience of the world pandemic and lockdown in particular, for posterity. I have always called the book "Lockdown Stories" but wondered at the end whether to re-name it "Pandemic Stories" as many people have described their whole experience. I decided to stick with the first one.

I began by asking friends and family what they thought of the idea. Some were more enthusiastic than others. Many said, "I didn't do anything. It will be boring." My response was that everyone's experience is valid. It then occurred to me that as an avid traveller, I had contacts across the globe, so I felt a perspective from different countries would make even more interesting reading. Hence, I have received contributions from the UK, of course and also from France, Spain, Australia, China, Canada, Dubai, New Zealand and the USA, with Sweden and India also making an appearance. I am conscious, however, that the chapters in this book do not encompass experiences from all walks of life. With hindsight I would like to have collected a broader spectrum of experience.

The same words are repeated in many of these stories: "unprecedented" and "Little did we know." How true! Several people commented on the sense of community they felt at the outset of the pandemic. Some said they found the process of writing their contribution cathartic, as did I. Re-reading these chapters always makes me feel emotional when I reflect on the writers' experiences. Some people said that they have forgotten what happened and the order of events in the last two years, so for them it was good to try to remember what had actually happened in their world as the pandemic unfolded. "Little did we know…"

I hope that you enjoy reading these stories and that some of the experiences of the authors may resonate with you. One thing is for certain: it changed our world irrevocably.

PART I

PANDEMIC STORIES

Some contributors chose to write slightly longer pieces and I have called these "Pandemic Stories". Some are set in the UK and several are from contributors from around the world.

Alone in Lockdown

by Joanna O'Donoghue

Jo lives and works in Norfolk in the UK. She is a self-employed education consultant and counsellor, currently also managing a team of mental health practitioners within the Norfolk Educational Psychology and Specialist Support Service. She had the idea for compiling people's experiences of lockdown as she has always wanted to write a book of some description. She felt that this may provide a cathartic experience for the contributors and also contribute to a little bit of history.

It was February 2020, and I had a trip booked to Laos, flying out via Vietnam. Everyone was talking about the mystery virus that was breaking out in China. I imagined that this would be contained in that part of the world, like SARS and Asian flu before it. I was asked more than once whether I had plans to cancel my trip. A friend of mine, a pharmacist said, "Keep washing your hands and don't touch your face." Another friend suggested taking First Defence before the flight to stop the germs getting up my nose. Little did we know what was about to unfold.

I went on the trip anyway. The plane was half empty and I was concerned that the man on the other side of the aisle kept coughing. When I arrived in Vientiane and checked in at the hotel, I was told that I could take a free disposable facemask each day. I thought that was quite funny and took a selfie of myself wearing it with a Facebook post status: "Hmm safe not safe? Didn't bother wearing it outside. Coughed and spluttered over for ten hours on the flight to Vietnam by the man opposite me. 'Horses 'and 'bolted' comes to mind."(February 20th, 2020.)

There were noticeably fewer tourists in Laos and the vendors in the night markets of Luang Prabang were desperate to sell their wares. Goodness knows how some of these people have survived for the last two years as their livelihoods depend on tourism.

The flight back home took me through an eerily deserted Vietnam airport. It was while I was sitting there waiting for my flight that my son called me to tell me the exciting news that his girlfriend was pregnant. An amazing surprise and a great beginning to 2020! The flight home was strange as I had a whole row of seats to myself. I kept washing my hands as instructed!

Returning to work after this holiday, people were talking about nothing else but the virus. I'm not sure I knew what its name was at that point. A colleague came to sit next to me in the office and thoroughly sprayed the workstation, the seat and the surrounding area with sanitizer. I almost expected her to give me a good spraying down as well and remember thinking she was being a bit over the top.

About two weeks later on the 16th March 2020, Boris Johnson announced that he would be implementing measures to halt the spread of the virus. My son announced that he and his girlfriend were leaving London and going to Sweden to stay with his girlfriend's parents, as they felt they might be safer there. My son was worrying about his cat Foxy, so I offered to drive to London and collect her. Evacuee cat! He later said that I begged him not to go, which I don't recall saying, but as I hugged them goodbye and headed back to Norfolk, I had an uneasy feeling in my gut.

By the end of March, over four thousand people had died in England within twenty-eight days of testing positive. The first lockdown began in England on 23rd March 2020. We thought it would be for three weeks. And so it unfolded; this was just the start of something, which would change our lives forever. Stay at home, we were told, work from home and do not have any unnecessary contact. We kept hearing about the old and the vulnerable and unfortunately for me, I fell into the latter category or possibly both! I have an autoimmune condition and had just started on a new drug, which worked by destroying the immune system. I realised that for my own safety and in this situation, which we didn't appear to know enough about, I should "isolate". This was the beginning of several months "isolating" and living alone in my house.

At first, three weeks seemed nothing and even quite a novelty. I had just started a new job managing a team of staff working in schools with children with social, emotional and mental health difficulties. Children had to quickly adapt to on-line learning, as did the teachers and only the children of key workers and vulnerable children attended school. We rapidly learned how to use Teams and work began on line and from home for me, as it did for many people. Offices were established in bedrooms and on kitchen tables. Many families, including some of my team members, were managing all of this in one small house. It was difficult to juggle working from home with on-line schooling, especially for those with very young children. In addition, all social contact dwindled to immediate families in the household, which presented further challenges for a lot of people. It suited some, who were happy to hunker down with their loved ones, but it left some people, including myself, very isolated and lonely.

Life took on a new pattern for me. The weather was kind, which meant getting outside for a walk was enjoyable and the only thing to do after staring at the screen all day. I started knitting for the baby and making lavish meals at the end of the day for myself. I even baked bread. I didn't visit supermarkets so my daughter ordered my shopping online and delivered it every week. Sometimes we had a ten-minute conversation in the car park standing far away from each other with no hugging allowed. People began to FaceTime and Zoom and that was one way of keeping in touch with friends and family. In the beginning this was enjoyable and I saw some friends more often on-line during this time than I had ever been able to keep up with them in person.

COVID-19 briefings happened daily at 5pm and the public watched the figures steadily rising, as the numbers of deaths grew daily. I can't remember at what point it was declared to be a world pandemic. The NHS was stretched and people stood on their doorsteps on Thursday nights to clap. It was impossible to get a doctor's appointment but I had to regularly visit the surgery for blood tests. This involved standing outside and waiting to be let in, my temperature taken and a whole rigmarole about safety, involving masks and lots of sanitizing and hand washing. I was having difficulty with the medication I had been prescribed, which was giving me worrying side effects and this was further complicated by the restrictions on hospital visits. More of that later.

The weeks passed. We all thought that the holidays we had booked in May and the summer of 2020 may still go ahead but it was looking increasingly unlikely as countries closed their borders in an attempt to contain this virus.

At this time my aunt was also becoming increasingly poorly. Having been diagnosed with Merkel Cell Carcinoma in 2018, a very rare form of cancer, she had received a course of radiotherapy, which had halted its deadly progress temporarily. Just before lockdown she had some complications related to this with a lump in her groin, which made it difficult for her to walk. She was admitted to a care home in January 2020. All across the country, care homes were closing their doors to protect the elderly and vulnerable and no visitors were allowed. I called from time to time and managed to speak to her on the phone. My sister who lived nearby was not allowed to visit between March and July. Sometimes my aunt's mood was very low and at other times she appeared more stoic.

As we approached the summer of 2020 there was promise of the easing of some restrictions. On 23rd June 2020, Boris Johnson announced that some changes would allow friends and family to see each other and from 4th July pubs, restaurants and hairdressers reopened under COVID-19 secure guidelines. At last I could get a haircut! Two households could meet with social distancing in place. Meeting outside seemed safer and at last I was able to meet with my daughter and family for walks outside and even managed to celebrate my birthday in a restaurant. My son and his girlfriend returned from Sweden and visited Norfolk and the evacuee cat returned to London. As I missed having a cat around, I decided to adopt a rescue cat, Angel, who came to live with me in July and spent the first few weeks hiding from me.

Looking back at this time, it is sometimes difficult to remember the exact order of events but I think we all endeavoured to "follow the rules" whilst keeping ourselves safe and our mental health intact. During that summer I was able to visit the Midlands and stay in an Airbnb to help my sister begin to clear my aunt's house, as it was unlikely that she would ever leave the care home. She had unfortunately fallen and broken her hip and had been admitted to hospital in March where she caught COVID-19. This had complicated matters immensely and she ended up on a ward waiting for a hip replacement and as a result got an ungradable bedsore. After the operation she was returned to the care home in an ambulance where they wouldn't re-admit her because she was still testing positive for COVID-19. All of these events were very traumatic for someone in their nineties and in the last months of her life. I managed to visit on August 10th 2020 and my sister and I stood behind a fence outside the care home about six feet away from her as she sat in her wheelchair. A vestige of her feisty nature remained but she became very agitated when the carer did not arrive to take her back at the allotted time. That was the last time I saw her. No hug goodbye, just a wave.

In August the family managed to rent a cottage for a week. Staycations had become "de rigeur." We enjoyed some family time and it felt as if maybe things were turning a corner. Unfortunately, however, as we entered the autumn of 2020, there were warnings that restrictions may be reinstated.

In September 2020 the UK's COVID-19 alert was raised to Level 4 (second highest level of threat to our health service being able to cope) and further restrictions were announced on 24th September to attempt to reduce the level and minimise damage to lives and livelihoods. Restrictions included "the rule of six", which meant that no more than six people could meet either indoors or outside. Regional tiers were introduced and travel was discouraged between regions as some areas of the country had higher levels of infection than others. Statistics showed that this virus was now taking hold in other age groups and hospital admissions were increasing again. The concern was that with the colder weather and people being indoors the transmission rates would increase. Working from home continued to be the norm, face coverings had to be worn and the rule of six applied. Numbers at weddings and funerals were restricted. A second national lockdown was brought in as a "firebreak" to slow the rise in hospital admissions.

I continued to work from home and school visits from my team recommenced with very strict risk assessments in place but most of the work had to be carried out remotely. Some schools were reluctant to have visitors and professional workers in at this time. Like NHS workers, teachers were also under enormous pressure. The issue of children's mental health and the impact this whole situation was having on their learning as well as their social and emotional development, was obvious. Resources were compiled, advice given and support to all schools continued in various guises. What of my own mental health at this time? My super–resilience was beginning to waver at times I have to say. Work kept me focussed. As a gregarious person I was missing my active social life and travelling. I struggled with not being able to physically hug and touch my children and grandchildren and this made me sad. My health was deteriorating as each new drug didn't seem to work and my weakened immune system left me feeling very afraid.

Two family events marked this time. My aunt died on October 3rd alone in the care home and my grandson was born on the night of October 27th. A death and a birth, which aptly illustrated the circle of life and brought tears of sadness and tears of joy. I was unable to attend my aunt's funeral but watched it streamed live from the crematorium. My daughter and I held hands over the laptop and cried at the song, "Over the Rainbow" at the end. My son watched it from the hospital bedside, as his son had been born thirty- six hours before.

My grandson's birth was a joy within the family and lifted everyone's spirits enormously. He entered the world by emergency C-Section after a long and painful labour for his mother. As restrictions were temporarily lifted in some areas, I managed a quick visit to see him and hold him in my arms when he was just two weeks old. I know how lucky I was, as so many grandparents had been separated from their grandchildren for so long, especially those with families abroad who did not know when their next meeting would be.

Christmas approached and it was looking as if more restrictions would be imposed. Sections of the country with high rates of infection were placed into a tiered system and specific guidelines were issued covering Christmas. My son and family visited before Christmas and we ate a very chilly take away meal from a restaurant in my daughter's garden. The food became cold after a couple of minutes and our fingers were numb. My son and his girlfriend left that Sunday, as they were desperate to get to Sweden to see her parents with the new baby. This was always in the balance but they made it.

My health situation took a massive downturn that night and I ended up in Accident and Emergency (A&E.) I had been prescribed a biologic medication and had been injecting it every two weeks since September. I had been called by the hospital as there was concern about my liver function and I was instructed to stop taking it immediately. This seemed a bit late as it was in my system. It started with a pain in my hand and it spread to my arms until I was almost screaming with the pain. The staff at A and E were puzzled but were very reluctant to admit me as there were such high levels of COVID-19 in the hospital and I had a very weakened immune system. I was given morphine and sent home with an appointment for an MRI scan the next morning. Several days of intense pain followed as the pain travelled to all parts of my body and ended in another trip to A and E early on Christmas morning. I remember the irritated and overworked doctor asking me what I thought they could do for me and I tearfully said, "Tell me I'm not dying." A bit dramatic but it was a very scary experience. Eventually it all calmed down and I am convinced it was a reaction to the sudden withdrawal from the medication, although my consultant begs to differ.

Christmas came and went. My son proposed to his girlfriend on one knee by the lake in Sweden where her parents live and I received a wobbly video of the event filmed by her parents. And so 2020 drew to a close. What started as three weeks had turned into months. The whole world was realising that this was far from over and there was more ahead on this strange and weird journey that had begun with a news item in the early part of the year. The world and our place in it had been turned upside down. We didn't know what 2021 had in store at that point.

Facebook post. 30th December 2020: "The trouble with being ill in bed is that you sometimes do some on-line shopping that you wouldn't usually do. So... I bought one of those Facebook albums of your year in print. I felt that I wanted to capture something of this year. I haven't got it yet but just looked at it online and realised that actually this year has been quite special in many ways. Lots of photos of fabulous times with family, and a few friends, some great travel photos and photos of my top ten books (Facebook challenge during lockdown), some spectacular walks and scenery in Norfolk and Suffolk and some great pictures of food. We have had a death and a birth in the family and also an engagement. I now have THREE grandchildren, one of whom I didn't have this time last year. I got a new rescue cat, Angel, who is a beaut. My "new" job that I started in January has been great despite having to fulfil most of it remotely but I have been able to work with some fantastic colleagues ("Awesome SEMH Team"). I've sold my house and will be moving in 2021 if things go to plan. I've ended on a bad note health-wise but will fight back. So I'm looking into 2021 with hope in my heart. Wishing an (early) Happy New Year to Facebook friends near and far. Fingers crossed that next year is a good one for you all!"

2021 brought new challenges. Due to the speed of transmission and the pressure on hospitals, we entered another lockdown on 4th January. The "big vaccination programme" began and England appeared to be ahead of the game on this. As a vulnerable person, I received my first vaccination in February 2021. Topics of conversation centred on, "Did you have AstraZeneca or Pfizer?" "Did you have side effects?" I didn't have any side effects but found out later that this was probably because of my weakened immune system. Schools returned to remote learning and the streets were once again eerily quiet in Norwich.

It seemed as the year rolled by that we were going to have to live with this virus. The economy was suffering, many businesses had closed with more and more shops on the main two shopping streets of Norwich closing their doors and boarding up. People's mental health was high on the agenda and in view of this, my job kept me busy. Tourism had taken a battering and I wondered whether I would ever be able to travel again. It was difficult to stay upbeat.

Towards the end of the year, new variants emerged, Delta and Omicron, which didn't seem as deadly but spread like wildfire. Cases of Long Covid emerged and affected my immediate family and there is still little known about this or how long it will persist for. As we approached another Christmas, it looked as if Boris Johnson would lift restrictions and allow people to enjoy time with their families this year, although we all feared where this would lead as we entered the year of 2022. Now it is a case of who do you know who hasn't had COVID-19, rather than who do you know who has had it? My immediate family have now all succumbed. I have escaped thus far and two weeks ago, I received my second booster.

We are two years down the line at the time of writing this (March 2022). Sometimes it feels like a bad dream that I just can't escape from. The effects worldwide have been catastrophic for many people and within my own network of family and friends have been challenging. And now, just as we were beginning to feel as if we were moving forward, we have another fear to deal with, as the horror of Russia invading the Ukraine is unravelling before our eyes.

.

Before the Pandemic
by Sean

Sean is a secondary school English teacher and Head of Department who lives in Cambridge with his wife and son. His experience of the pandemic began in Shanghai during a two-year teaching contract at an international school there. Sean enjoys writing fiction for young adults, slacklining and taekwondo.

On Sunday 26th January 2020, my wife and I received an email from the international school we were working at in Shanghai to say that the school was closing.

At the time of the email, we were on holiday in Thailand. I'd just completed a diving course and was excited about the thought of taking it up as a new hobby. My son, wet from his swim in the pool, was bounding around the camping pod we'd hired on a beach in Phuket. It was the perfect holiday.

But the email confirmed the rumours that we'd been picking up from Chinese social media and from the noises being made by tour guides in Thailand, warning us to stay away from Chinese tourists. COVID-19 was a thing and it was starting to spread. The Chinese government had ordered our school to close and so we'd have to set work virtually for our students for the next two weeks.

It is odd to recall how blasé we were about it at the time. We had just enough Internet connection to set a few days' worth of work for our students, enough to get us back home and settled into a routine before continuing the holiday with crazy golf, beach beers and swimming.

Anxious to avoid two boring weeks of lockdown in our small Shanghai apartment, we decided to fly back to the UK the following week. It was only as we boarded the flight from Thailand back to Shanghai that the gravity of the situation became clear. During the pre-flight checks, our flight attendant warned us that Shanghai was closing imminently and that if we wanted to get out of the city, we needed to do so fast. As the plane taxied along the runway, we managed to change our flights to leave Shanghai the following day.

We landed in Shanghai at 3am after some delays. This was now the early hours of January 29th 2020. We got back to the apartment and combined packing for England with setting adequate work for our students. By now the school closure had been extended so the initial work we had lined up needed to be changed. It was an anxious day spent refreshing the news app through our VPN as more and more airlines closed down their Shanghai operations. The view from our bedroom window, usually a blanket of cars spread across twelve lanes of Shanghai traffic, was eerily silent. It felt like the scene from a disaster movie. The roads were completely empty and no one stood waiting at the pedestrian crossings.

My diary entry for this day reads, "BA announced during the day that it has suspended its service to China and the FCO's advice is now to avoid travel to Mainland China. Hard to know what is hysteria and what is legitimate concern – there certainly seems to be no let-up in the speed of the virus." By the time we got to the airport queue that evening, our Turkish Airlines flight was amongst the last to leave Shanghai. The check-in queue was slow and weighted heavily with nervous anticipation; with so much of the airport deserted, no one really knew if the flight was actually going to make it off the runway in time.

But it did and when we landed at Istanbul for our changeover, we were met with TV cameras and reporters who appeared to us to be reporting on the now obvious disruption to travel.

Arriving in the UK felt very strange indeed. It was a country that had just received its first flight from Wuhan. Images of those evacuated Brits taken in coaches to RAF Brize Norton topped the news headlines as we sat in my parents' living room in the South London suburbs feeling a strange mixture of guilt and relief.

Our lockdown story therefore comes in the weeks before the British lockdown actually started. It was an intensely stressful period of time in that it was absolutely unprecedented. Neither my wife nor I could offer any solutions to the situation we were in and, with the rest of the country effectively continuing as normal, we felt very much like outsiders. We were teaching online in Chinese time (albeit slightly altered to accommodate all the international teachers who had found themselves stranded all over the globe) whilst the rest of the country seemed oblivious to anything other than a virus with "flu-like symptoms". Our stress and anxiety was very much compounded by our concern for our eight-year-old son who was now missing out on school. We started with a strict routine for him to be able to carry on with home-learning whilst my wife and I taught our lessons online, but with our own teaching commitments, this quickly became untenable and we knew that we would have to do something different. However, slinking about in the middle of the day with a school-age child who was very obviously not in school, whilst all the time trying not to mention too loudly that we'd come from China was proving something of a challenge! There was no way of getting him into his previous British school which was fifty miles away in Cambridge and the school near my parents' home in South London was full. In any case, each time we tried to explain our situation, we were met with sideways glances and an understandable shuffling backwards. He would just have to sneak in next to us in the library and entertain himself whilst we hooked on to whatever free Wi-Fi was available. Wherever possible, we tried to capitalise on a city that was both open and full of opportunity. We have an excellent photograph of our son making notes in the Tutankhamun exhibition in a practically empty Saatchi gallery. We used the local swimming baths for his PE lessons and scooted about the park quite a lot, all the time feeling like naughty students skipping school.

But by the middle of March, about a week before the UK lockdown was announced, we had to face the decision that we'd been agonising over since we'd left: whether or not to return to Shanghai. The official message coming from the school's management was that life in Shanghai was now beginning to return to normal and that we must return ready for the school's imminent reopening. The Shanghainese were emerging from lockdown and pubs and restaurants were opening up to those who could prove they had undergone the requisite period of quarantine: the virus was losing. In my desk drawer at home, I still have two sealed letters: one to my wife and one to my son, to be opened in the event that I had to leave them in the UK to return to work out the remaining four months of our contract without them. Writing this now, that doesn't seem like such a big deal. But at the very start of a pandemic, when there was a very real threat of being removed to centralised government quarantine in Shanghai, when the death rate was steadily climbing and no one knew when or if there would be any sort of vaccine, that felt like quite a scary thing to do.

In the end, we decided to travel as a family and return to Shanghai together. And that was terrifying. We were travelling against the advice of the FCO and against the advice of our friends and family. But our home, our possessions, our jobs, our son's school, in fact our whole life at the time was back in Shanghai.

My father drove us to the airport on St Patrick's Day. We said our goodbyes and he left us to travel on to what would be the last work meeting of his career, as the guidance at the time was for the over seventies to stay at home. COVID-19 had both forced and eclipsed his retirement.

Our journey from London to Shanghai took thirty-nine and a half hours and can be mostly defined by queues and fear. We changed at Bangkok where the health screening began in earnest, although mainly just temperature checks at this point. By the time we landed in Shanghai, passengers were being called off the plane one-at-a-time. This was the bit that frightened us the most. We knew of colleagues who had been separated from their children at this juncture to be taken to "facilities" if they tested positive.

We wound our way through a maze of bewildering queues, managed with temporary airport barriers and screens. We did our best to follow the instructions being issued in Mandarin by people wearing multiple layers of hermetically sealed protection suits which were all dripping on the inside with condensation in the heat. Once through the infrared temperature checks at passport control, we received a large yellow sticker on the front of our passports to indicate we'd arrived from a "High Risk" country. From here, we were directed towards makeshift booths where we were met by more officials in hazmat suits and funnelled through different queues dependent on which region of Shanghai you were living in.

There was a bewildering amount of paperwork and, once completed, we were taken by bus to a school gymnasium, which was now repurposed as a testing centre. This was our first experience of a COVID-19 test. And it was grim. The nurse who tried to poke my brains out with a swab was quite taken aback by my involuntary gag reflex and at 2am, we were shown to our camp beds in the middle of the hall, illuminated by the unforgiving strip lighting of a sports hall.

We waited some three hours or so for the results to come back negative. It's quite difficult to express how nerve-wracking, confusing and disorientating those three hours were. One by one, people's names were called out and people left the gym. Eventually, our names were called and we received our negative tests results. We were loaded onto another coach and taken by police escort through Shanghai and back to our compound. By now, with China claiming some control over the virus, there was a palpable fear of westerners arriving into the city and it seemed as though we were going to be turned away at the gates, but with proof of negative tests and yet more temperature checks, we were allowed through and escorted to our apartment. And so for us, Quarantine Day One began on the 19th March, 2020 still four days before the UK announced its lockdown. A magnetic seal was installed on our door which activated a visit from a man in a hazmat suit when opened, something we discovered when we put the rubbish out. A banner with the words "Home Quarantine" emblazoned in Mandarin was pasted to the outside of our front door and I wondered if a red X wouldn't have been more effective. A nurse visited twice a day to take our temperature and an automated phone call tracked our whereabouts once a day.

In the middle of our fourteen-day quarantine, it was my wife's birthday. I'd packed some balloons and a murder mystery game before we left England. We all dressed up and had a mini lockdown party but it didn't do much to abate the anxiety felt that, at any moment, should anyone else on either of the flights we had boarded since leaving the UK have tested positive, then we too would have been collected and taken to centralised quarantine. It was a long and intense fourteen days.

Thankfully, despite a terrifyingly false alarm when the police came to talk to someone else on our floor on Day Thirteen, we received our green QR health codes on Thursday 2nd April. We were allowed out of our apartment and back into a Shanghai that felt quite normal: if you could ignore the temperature checks at the entrance to every shop and restaurant; the requirement to have a green QR health code available at all times on your phone and the constant thought that if you came into contact with anyone who tested positive, you could be collected by the authorities.

We remained in Shanghai for about four months after this, during which time things began to feel quite 'normal' with shops, restaurants, schools and even trampoline parks open for business. Although our travel within China was heavily restricted, we valued the opportunities to be out with friends in the city whilst the UK was experiencing its first lockdown. In September 2020 we returned to teaching in the UK and, having experienced an extended period of online teaching, we were well prepared for what was to happen next!

Shanghai: the best of times, the worst of times.

The author is English and lives in Miami with her husband and two children from where she runs an online business. The family moved to Shanghai in the summer of 2017 for a two-year contract. In the summer of 2019 they opted to extend the contract to summer 2022.

I can't really remember when I first heard about COVID-19 or the Coronavirus as we called it back then. I had been living with my husband and two daughters in Shanghai for two and a half years and we loved it. We travelled whenever there was a school holiday (to amazing places like Japan, Australia, New Zealand, Cambodia and Thailand) and explored Shanghai every weekend. We had a wonderful group of mainly expat friends and my husband's company paid for us to come home to the US or the UK twice a year. Our daughters attended a British international school which they loved, while I enjoyed being part of the multi-cultural school community and helping to organize events.

In January of 2020 we were flying from Shanghai back to Florida for the Chinese New Year holiday. My husband had to stay for a couple more days and was joining us later that week. COVID-19 must have been emerging in Wuhan at that point but none of us expats took anything more than suitcases packed for a two-week trip when we left Shanghai, so I suppose we assumed it would blow over. Things must have progressed very quickly because a few days later my husband cancelled his flight to the US as things started to get very difficult for his travel company. I remember sitting in the Airbnb apartment we were renting by the sea listening to him in total panic as his company's most profitable time of the year became their least profitable in a matter of hours. All travel was banned in China and soon the frightening images and videos of Wuhan were all over the news.

We decided that the girls and I should stay in the US for the time being. Online school started in a very chaotic way, we managed it the best we could while staying at my in-laws in Florida and then my sister-in-law's house in Atlanta. The girls' prolonged time with their cousins was one of the COVID-19 highlights, despite the worry about my husband back in China and the huge amounts of schoolwork coming their way. At this time Shanghai never went into lockdown. I think there were less than a hundred cases in early 2020, but the city was a pretty miserable place to be alone in at that time. Pollution levels were always worse in the winter. It was cold and dreary and the streets were empty as everyone was petrified of this new mystery virus. I think people had suffered a lot during the SARS outbreak and this was still fresh in their memories. In contrast, things were normal in the US apart from our living situation and tackling E-learning. Basically trying to kill time, we got a good deal on a cruise through my husband's company and decided to spend a week at sea. I was feeling a bit sorry for myself, buried in print outs from school and not sure what we would do next. I remember telling our story to the crew on board countless times and of course now realise the irony of that. It must have been a matter of weeks before they would be stranded at sea, quarantined for several months.

Through all this I was constantly in touch with my group of eight best friends from Shanghai. We have a WeChat (Chinese messaging app) group and supported each other through this tough time. We had all left Shanghai for the holiday and were stranded in different parts of the world, wondering what to do as the situation in China got stranger and it didn't seem a good idea to return 'home'. In mid-February I was considering flying to the UK and enrolling my younger daughter in the village school I went to as a child. Meanwhile, unbeknownst to us all, COVID-19 was creeping closer to everyone. Finally we made the decision to return to China. Because of all the images of people in hazmat suits and the extreme situation in Wuhan, people thought we were crazy. My husband however, always a risk-taker and usually right, convinced me to take the girls back. I was nervous but knew it also wasn't fair for him to be there alone and I trust his instincts. We flew from Atlanta to Chicago and then to Japan. In Tokyo, where COVID-19 had begun to emerge, we were fully masked and frequently hand sanitizing. From Tokyo to Shanghai we were the only people in our cabin on the plane and the flight attendants were in hazmats.

We landed in Shanghai on February 27th 2020 and breezed through a deserted airport. When we arrived at our apartment, one of the lovely staff from our compound asked if we thought we should quarantine. I practically laughed in his face as we had come from the outside world where COVID-19 didn't exist. On February 29th I turned 44 and the four of us had dinner at my favourite Italian restaurant. The restaurant is usually packed but this time there were around eight tables of diners and the usually bustling street below was empty. The next few weeks were quiet, things gradually re-opened and conditions began to reverse as China seemed to have 'beaten' COVID-19. We were the only people I know that made it into China with no testing or quarantine. As the virus quickly spread around the world the policies for entering Shanghai changed daily. One friend made it back and was advised to quarantine. We met for a coffee on the second day and noticed a colleague from her office snapping a photo of her, as she was breaking the unofficial rules. She got nervous and stayed at home for the rest of the ten days. As COVID-19 took hold around the world, foreigners began to be seen as a threat (I'm sure an attitude exacerbated by the media) and we got strange looks wherever we went. This was in contrast to the way we were usually treated; Chinese people were generally very welcoming to us and sweet to our daughters. Another friend returned from the UK by which time airport testing and home quarantine for two weeks (with an alarm connected to the neighbourhood committee on their door) was mandatory. Other friends were scrambling to come back to Shanghai before the situation got worse overseas, but flights were difficult to secure. It was around the end of March 2020 that China closed their borders and it became virtually impossible for anyone to return.

The girls were still doing school from home, but by this point all the lessons were live online and much more manageable. It wasn't long before schools were allowed to open again and life went back to normal. Friends overseas gradually assembled the massive amounts of paperwork and permissions to allow them to return to Shanghai and those of us already back delivered them supplies during quarantine, which was now an obligatory two weeks in a government designated hotel with COVID-19 tests every day.

The next eighteen months were actually quite wonderful. There were huge downsides....we couldn't travel outside the country which led to none of us seeing our families for two and a half years, and business for my husband's company never recovered in China. But in comparison with the rest of the world we led very normal lives for the second part of 2020 and 2021. Our group of friends spent a lot of time together, taking holidays in beautiful parts of China we would never have visited otherwise. We made the most of two Christmas and New Year holidays and all grew very close. The children loved being together constantly and I loved having such a close group of female friends. I stayed in constant contact with my family with regular calls, Skyping and emails. I was definitely worried about them as COVID-19 got worse and then wouldn't go away, but I knew they were comfortable at home and being cautious. I know that I'll never properly understand what that awful, never-ending period of lockdown was like for the rest of the world.

My husband's Shanghai contract coming to an end in the summer of 2022 had been planned for a while so we began to prepare slowly. In the autumn of 2021 we applied for schools for the girls back in the US and my older daughter took the Secondary School Admission Test (SSAT) entrance exam in Shanghai. I notified the people renting our house in Florida that my husband would be coming back in February to take up a new position at his company, although the girls and I planned to stay to finish the school year. We hadn't been to Beijing yet so we were planning to take a trip to the Great Wall and tick off other Shanghai 'bucket list' items that we hadn't yet found time to do during our five years in the city.

My husband left Shanghai at the end of February 2022; somehow he has evaded all lockdowns and this time was no different! Cases of the ultra-transmittable Delta variant had begun to emerge in the city and on a Thursday shortly after he left, the girls were held at school for mandatory testing. One student was a second-tier contact of a COVID-19-case but fortunately the school all tested negative and they finally got home at 11pm. The next day I felt too nervous to send them to school; the consequences for testing positive were becoming clear and I didn't want to risk that. The girls stayed home for the day as I wanted to see how things progressed over the weekend, and they never went back. This is one of the aspects of the following couple of months that makes me the saddest. They never got to say goodbye to teachers and friends; we never stepped foot on campus again. My older daughter's belongings were still in her locker and we never got them back. This was the beginning of our final two months in China, which ended so differently from what I'd had in mind.

Sporadic and sudden lockdowns began to spread. I cancelled a hair appointment as people began to get shut in malls overnight if a COVID-19 case had passed through. The government announced that schools must move online and we all started to feel uneasy. Of course by this point nobody was afraid of the virus itself but the consequences of testing positive were fairly extreme. As case numbers rose the number of quarantine hotels grew until they ran out of space. The next stage was the opening of massive quarantine sites set up in convention centres and anywhere else that could hold rows and rows of beds. Even one of the Olympic aquatic centres was used, with the water drained from the pool to make way for beds.

Life in the city continued in a fairly normal way. People had, to some extent, got over their fear of the virus knowing from the outside world that, for most, the symptoms weren't as severe as they used to be.

At the end of March 2022 the Shanghai government announced a staggered four-day lockdown to try to control the spread of the virus. The city is divided into two main sections; Pudong to the east of the river and Puxi, to the west. The lockdown in Pudong went into effect while people were sleeping so they had no chance to gather supplies or prepare. If the lockdown had been four days, as was promised, most people would have been able to manage well. In Puxi, where we lived, we were lucky to have a few days' notice. I placed two large grocery orders online to be delivered in the days leading up to the lockdown.

Unfortunately the store was ordered to cease operations the day before the lockdown which meant I didn't receive my shopping. I spent the night before lockdown cycling to friends' houses in the rain to gather any supplies they could spare. The city was deserted, barricades had begun to be set up, quite in contrast with the bustling scenes in the days leading up to this point, as people scrambled to buy vegetables and meat. The shelves of all the shops were empty by the day before lockdown.

This period and the beginning of lockdown were a bit like when a hurricane hits Florida. It is a novelty to start off with partly because you think it's no more than an inconvenience and the break from normal routines is quite appreciated. But then when things began to feel scary and food was hard to come by the novelty wore off quickly. When the promised end of lockdown came and went people began to get annoyed but we still had plenty of food and assumed that the lockdown would end soon. We started being asked to go out to the playground of our compound for daily COVID-19 tests. Any positive cases were taken away to the huge quarantine centres. As it became clear that these places were far from pleasant we all felt more paranoid that we could also test positive. The main worry for me was hearing about children being separated from their parents. The rules seemed to change every day and rumours circulated constantly. We used WeChat to stay in touch with each other and formed many different groups to support each other. I was part of an 'Americans Leaving Shanghai' group consisting of people trying to navigate how to leave the city under such strict lockdown. Our compound also formed two groups, one for general discussions and the other on food procurement.

Food became an issue after a week or so. All shops and delivery services had been ordered to cease operations. A handful were allowed to open so I went through a period of waking up at 5am to try to get one of the delivery slots available on one of the Chinese delivery apps. I never really managed to and it was unclear how those shops were operating, if at all. The various chat groups were full of discussions about how people had managed to get one of the elusive deliveries, even if it was just some milk and a kilo of tomatoes. Prices went through the roof and soon 'group buys' became a normal part of life. Shops and farmers that were allowed to operate and deliver worked out that it would be much more worthwhile to sell huge amounts of food rather than individual orders (I think they may have only been allowed to deliver to a few addresses a day). Our compound chat was full of people organising group buys for items such as bread, vegetables and rice. As delivery would take three or four days I started to panic-buy whatever was available each day. It meant I ended up with sixty eggs at one point as everything had to be bought in bulk and my neighbours were swimming in eggs too! The memes of piles of eggs, tomatoes and apples circulated quickly.

The girls continued with online school and we only left our apartment for daily COVID-19 tests. We could get called for them at any time and, as case numbers went up, I continued to feel nervous that testing positive was a real possibility. I heard of a few people taken from our compound during this time but it didn't happen to any of my close friends. The girls and I were very lucky to have a ground floor apartment and a garden. Apparently someone in the building opposite complained that we were spending time outside but I totally ignored that! The government started delivering food rations which was always a source of amusement. My younger daughter grabbed two bags from outside our door one day saying 'They gave us tons of carrots!'. On closer inspection we realised that the bags in fact contained two chickens, head and feet included. Fortunately we were never desperate enough for me to have to attempt a de-heading.

The staff of our compound who were there at the beginning of the 'four day' lockdown weren't allowed to leave (nobody in the city was allowed to enter or leave a community during this time) and took such good care of the residents. They were away from their families for almost two months and worked incredibly hard distributing the huge food deliveries that came in and coordinating the mandated PCR tests. A very organised group of neighbours worked to coordinate the group purchases, the trainers at our gym led online classes from their apartments and our school's teachers did an incredible job of teaching online under what were incredibly difficult circumstances.

Gradually, a few friends in smaller neighbourhoods began to get released due to their buildings having no positive cases for several weeks. We never really knew why but we never got out. However, we were eventually allowed to leave our apartments and roam freely within our gated compound. This was a much easier time, especially for my younger daughter who finished her online school at 2.30 and then ran free with her friends until it got dark. We would have picnics and drinks with neighbours, most of whom I didn't know before lockdown. My 'free' friends made pizza and delivered it to our gate, and one day we even met for drinks through my gate, until the police came and put an end to our get-together.

Throughout this time I was gradually packing our apartment and the sadness of leaving Shanghai was never lessened by this stressful experience. I knew it was time to leave, however nobody knew when the lockdown would end and even after that, everybody was nervous that this could happen all over again at any time. We were fortunate and despite some worrying moments, I always knew that there were people in much worse situations, locked in tiny dark apartments, possibly without the resources and knowledge to get much needed food and medical supplies.

The only time we saw the streets of Shanghai again was the day before we flew out of the city. We went to a designated hospital for a PCR test so we could enter the airport. I asked our driver to drop us off a few streets from our apartment so we could have a walk and visit friends. We hugged two favourite families on their doorsteps and one of my friends through her gate. The streets were still deserted (six weeks into lockdown) with strange blue barriers in place on all our most-loved streets. Some were around doorways to prevent people leaving, and others in random places not really stopping anyone from going anywhere.

The next day the girls and I loaded up our twelve suitcases and said very sad goodbyes to our neighbours and the staff of our compound. Even with things the way they were it was very hard to leave. We all loved Shanghai so much but for most people this situation became too overwhelming to live with. Out of eight of my friends, five of us have now left Shanghai permanently. My older daughter's friends have all left their school and most have left China.

Ten weeks after leaving Shanghai our belongings are still there, stuck in a huge backlog of expat shipments waiting to leave China. Three days after touching down in Florida we all tested positive. Our COVID-19 experience was now complete, and I felt great relief that the positive test meant nothing more than staying at home to recover.

Funerals in times of COVID-19

by Rita-Marie Lenton

Rita-Marie grew up in rural Queensland, Australia where she lives with her husband, David and high-maintenance, media-savvy pet cat, "Miss Sweetie." Rita-Marie has had twenty-one years in a fascinating career as a funeral director and crematorium manager. Since retiring from her career she is still involved in funerals but on a more spiritual level, as a funeral Celebrant.

Rita-Marie is a contributing author and has also authored her own book. Her own life story is one of triumphing over adversity and the gift of forgiveness.

In the January of 2020, COVID-19 had come to our shores. I wasn't overly concerned, as I thought this was to be another virus that the country prepared for by putting protocols in place. In my twenty-one-year career as a funeral director and crematorium manager, I had experienced bird flu, swine flu, Creutzfeldt -Jakob Disease (CJD) SARS and many more.

All funeral companies already had strict infection controls around dealing with the deceased. At the onset of COVID-19, they became stricter.

Moving into February 2020, things were beginning to become real and panic was starting to set in around the country. Then in March 2020, came the mandates and paranoia that were to continue over the next few years.

The first time I had pause for thought was when we organised with a family for a direct cremation. They were allowed a viewing in our viewing room with only ten people in attendance, as this was the mandated number of people permitted at our venue for a funeral. There was an elderly couple in the midst and I saw the gentleman pause at the drink dispenser. When I approached him to see if he required any help, he said, "Yes, could you pour me a drink as I am not supposed to touch anything." This is when he admitted to returning back from overseas the night before. What the hell? When I asked why he and his wife were not in quarantine the reply came, " It is all right, we don't feel sick."

The company started to implement the guidelines of no more than two people in the office at a time. No-one was to enter the building without a mask and sanitising stations were set up at every entrance. Staff were required to be separated, to have their lunch at either their desk or were only allowed one at a time in the lunchroom.

The staff became targets, because they were tasked with monitoring how many people would be in the grounds at any one time, as it was necessary to stick to the government mandates. I became the barrier that stood between my staff and the angry grieving families as we had to place restrictions on how many people could visit our facility. My job was to protect the company and my staff.

As the manager, it was my job to ensure other funeral companies stuck to the protocols in place, making sure they kept their numbers within the permitted limits. As funeral directors and crematorium staff, we didn't get to work from home and we turned up for work every day. People were still passing away so cremations and burials still had to go ahead.

I became hardened, which made me seem uncaring and cold. Every day it was getting harder and harder to get up and go into work. I had lost my passion.

As the months passed, the funeral numbers had started to increase, which allowed more people to attend services. We still had to have protocols around how many could sit in the chapel and how many could be outside and then we had to introduce the check-in app. "Oh what fun!" says I with tongue-in-cheek.

Funeral attendance numbers went up and down like a yo-yo. The challenge we faced every day was just where the mandates were and how many could attend a funeral service. A few years before, the company had put in place the ability to record the service for families and we went about organising live-streaming the service over the Internet.

At the beginning of the lockdowns, the hardest part of organising one of the funerals, was for that of a young lad who had been murdered and having to tell his parents that only eight people could attend his funeral. The mother was devastated, the father was extremely angry and to make matters worse, the police were in attendance, so they could make sure no one else turned up for the service.

Mandates changed around the number of people who could attend a funeral over the next two years and each day you felt as if you were on a knife-edge. The government would change the rules daily. It became a funeral director's nightmare, as we had to continually inform families that there could only be a certain number of people at a service. The fun challenge was when we could finally have up to one hundred at a service, with only thirty sitting inside the chapel. Who got to decide? The family would give us a list and as funeral directors at the door, we had to check the names off. This sometimes led to some very angry mourners who felt they should be allow inside the chapel.

Those inside the chapel had to sit 1.5 metres apart. This was a joke as no-one stuck to what was supposed to happen. At one of the funerals I had arranged, I had to go to the mourners and ask them to sit apart. They said, "It is okay, we are from the same family." " However," I answered, "You don't all live in the same state so you must adhere to the mandate please."

If it wasn't the government changing the rules, it was the management so I felt pulled in all directions. Even being able to visit my grandchildren was not allowed as they lived across the border in New South Wales, and I started to feel isolated, as I was unable to catch up with friends outside of work. The complaints kept coming. I decided that after twenty-one years of service in a career I loved, I could no longer do it. The emotional roller coaster was just too much. So, on the 30th September 2021, I closed the door on my career.

Whilst I was one of the fortunate ones never to contract COVID-19, as a long-term allergy sufferer, the effects of the pandemic have left me with a constant feeling of anxiety. Friends will prefer if I don't visit if I have a runny nose, so isolation is still something I struggle with. I find going to the doctor a chore, especially if my sinuses become infected from my allergies and my doctor will insist on a COVID-19 PCR test before she even allows me to go to the clinic. I carry masks and sanitiser everywhere I go and emotionally I continue to become anxious going out to shops and events around a large number of people.

Distance	Pace		Achievements
4.55 mi	10:32 /mi		🏅 🏅 🏅 13

Spain in the time of COVID-19
by Sam

Sam (not his real name) is a Spanish graduate from the UK, who has worked in Barcelona and Marbella off and on for many years. He is single and was in his late thirties at the start of the pandemic.

Scene One:

My COVID-19 story really began sitting in a coffee house in Barcelona. It was a Friday in mid-February 2020 and I had just completed my customary three to four mile run after work. I was listening to the tail end of 'PM' on BBC Sounds' Radio 4.

This stalwart of my daily routine enabled me to keep abreast of UK and BBC news reporting on wider global events. Luckily, it started an hour later than in the UK due to Spanish time being an hour ahead. This was very useful for me as it coincided with finishing work and cracking on with the almost daily 'bomb-around-town', before finally relaxing for the day.

It was here that evening that I pondered the worsening developments in Italy over my headphones. I was hearing about the rumoured to be infamous COVID-19, unknown but to a handful of doctors, nurses, and scientists. Now, it was seemingly making its despicable and unrelenting way through large swathes of the Italian population in areas of Northern Italy, causing prescribed lockdowns in the areas most affected, as it did so.

I had followed the story from its early inception and noted almost daily (via my stints listening to 'PM'), that there had been scant real-time updates coming from the Chinese, other than the ominous entire shutdown of the large city of Wuhan. It was subsequently very disturbing to hear the chaos now afflicting Italy.

I wondered what Spain would do, given fears over a very recent large-scale football match that Spain had hosted, between themselves and the aforementioned Italians. I knew full well that the Spanish authorities tend not to apply legislation in half measures, especially if a direct threat to the state is perceived. Pondering all this, I headed back across Avenida Paral·lel, to my shared apartment at the foot of Montjuïc.

What I had not anticipated even at this stage though, was the complete change I'd be seeing in the coming days. In fact, some short days later my normal extremely vibrant and teeming 'work-break-out-area', in the bustling outdoor centre of the town's World Trade Centre offices down by the port, would be completely empty – with the exception of a group of twenty or so Spanish army personnel, each brandishing high calibre rifles. Quite the step change!

I had been part of the Disney Plus Account Management Team for Spain and the UK market. I was there on site and one of only a handful of people I had even seen that day, when we were all sent home with firm instructions to 'work from home' thereafter and, very ominously, 'until further notice'. We had though, each been afforded beforehand a company letter, explaining that if out on the street for any reason, we could offer this document to the various police forces and army personnel now vehemently patrolling the streets (a sight more synonymous with Franco's police state than modern day Spain). This letter was supposedly some sort of assurance to the powers that be, that this employee was out only as a last resort: that said employee's working hours meant they had to go to the office in a work emergency, and would only be doing so if for a vital work-related issue. In reality of course this letter was largely useless. Yet we had no choice but to risk it as evidence of an excuse, if we did have to run the gauntlet of returning to an all but empty office, for the one techy left alive, to fix our gear.

Otherwise the city's inhabitants were fully restricted to only one daily outing, and only for food and water. It was therefore not entirely lost on me that my 'essential work issue', and my entire reason for being out there, though certainly work related (i.e. a home PC system VPN breakdown) was not in any way within a sector we could sensibly call 'vital'. I was sure that health workers and other emergency services were certainly distinguishable from those working for 'Disney'!

This particular, 'hardware run to the office' was certainly what had created my sense of trepidation, especially on seeing the sight of the twenty 'tooled up blokes' with automatic weapons now doing reconnaissance all across the main courtyards of the building. This was for sure a giant sea-change from the normal one hundred and fifty odd people in the square for their lunch breaks, all working out of the various World Trade Centre company offices. This was a far cry from the latte sipping, 'bocadillo' baguette eating alumni of those offices, as they would have had their natters and gossip about the issues of the day, from behind a pair of sunglasses.

In fact nothing at all had been normal in the city for some days.The eerie quiet had spread like insomnia through an Amazonian village, until there was nothing but vacant schools, university buildings, streets, monuments, and business establishments all across this greater Barcelona area - a city of over three and a half million people. This was the external environment; my internal world was something quite different.

Scene Two:

My girlfriend is asking me to go directly to Carrefour...

We have been thrust into a situation where we now live together in her flat. Despite having my own, now deserted three-bedroom apartment, just fifteen minutes' walk away, lockdown quickly taught us the pointlessness of me staying over at my place, if it just means we have voluntarily separated ourselves. This, at a time when people are most alone and barred from socialising with anyone else. That, and the fact that she is scared to physically leave her building, results in me being a modern day 'hunter-gatherer' - flat sharer and her only provider of food!

We'd met after a couple of weeks of me being back in town for a new job. That was back in November 2019, which somehow feels like a lifetime ago now ....

I'd met her outside a small and very quirky Mexican restaurant in the Raval area, in the time before COVID-19. We had walked the bustling streets of Gothic, Raval, Gracia, Barcelonetta. I'd marvelled at her amazing and quite unrelenting walking speed and her ability to walk through a gap of between one, two or more people, completely unabated and often leaving me for dust. She would converse with her favoured stall keepers at the 'la bocaria' market off La Rambla, ordering only the best slabs of meats and cheeses from what was already an exemplary group of independent stalls. She could simultaneously negotiate, explain concepts, barter with traders, play tour guide, occasionally flirt, and wear black so much - to the point where she seemed more enigma than anything else. Half Basque and half Scottish, a lawyer by trade, her two sole favourite pastimes, were cooking in her home Basque style and techno (as long as the DJ met her highly demanding standards).

These types of exploits now seem like a yesterday that never existed or would never return in the same way ever again. April 2020... and the deserted streets were proof that the situation in Spain had reached a critical level, with a palpable sense of desperation in the air and over the air waves.

Citizens had all been given permission for just one person per household, to be permitted to go out once per day, but specifically only for essential food and water and for those items alone. People who owned a dog had permission to walk it once a day.

So she asks me to go directly to Carrefour...

This will involve navigating through some of the nearby narrow streets of the 'Raval' district, which borders 'Gothic' and avoiding unnecessary questions, and/or being stopped by passing, 'policia urbina', and for sure not loitering or being seen in fact to be too happy or too normalised, so as not to attract unwanted attention in these strange days. Nor was it permitted to be sitting anywhere stationary e.g. park benches are no longer for sitting on, and punishable with a fine and potentially arrest, upon refusal to get up!

"Hmmm, so if I'm picked up with any booze and not much food, and worse still no water, this could also be a problem" (I'd selfishly thought to myself, when these stipulations had originally be given to us)...

My girlfriend does not go out of her flat now: still able to teach some of her online English language classes to her group of younger law students, as well as individual classes to a handful of other adult professionals. This provides her with a focus and much needed outlet from the monotony of this military style city-wide lockdown.

Satisfied to be able to still teach her stuff, and with cooking as her passion, the other daily although awe-inspiring and patriotic routine we became accustomed to, was the 8pm daily city-wide clapping of the health workers of Spain. Shouts of "Bravo!" "Bravo!" "Bravo!" would be heard echoing across the city each night at the same time, whilst the thousands of us kept locked up in our flats became momentarily visible to each other as we clapped and kept each other going once each night at this time. Everyone joined in. In a city full of balconies of upwards of six or seven storeys it became quite a sight in itself and I have already internalised this memory. We lived a strange and at times dreamlike existence together within the confines of her Raval apartment, frequently taking videos of our cooking exploits, which we shared with family in the UK. Strange how quickly I became used to this new norm.

Hardly ever leaving the flat herself, one the few occasions we ventured out at the same time, we ensured we walked fifteen feet apart, so as not to attract trouble with police. So, it was in this context therefore, that I had largely assumed the role of daily hunter-gather, and would be heading out again shortly via the now completely deserted Bocaria market. She informs me of the specific food items to be bought for today's meal...

April winds its way on..
Days pass just like this..
Same daily routine..

Now it's a Saturday in mid-late April and I have been forced to use my 'unavoidable essential work-related issue' letter to make my way across town. The VPN function on my work PC has become unresponsive yet again and I've been told by Disney's Spanish partner company to go to an office where someone can look at it. This means taking the regularly patrolled and largely deserted metro across town. Now on my return leg and finally off the metro I make a mental note that it's a sunny day; bucking the trend of what had been an uncharacteristically overcast April - as if even El Nino himself was also seeking to emphasise the drastic nature of the city's plight.

I find myself deep in thought, until lifting my head up and finding that unconsciously I've taken a short cut through 'Calle Leitana' and am standing in the middle of the road halfway up La Rambla. I am looking down towards the harbour, and up towards Placa Cataluna. It is 16.10pm on Saturday, and I pause for no more than a moment, before realising that there is not one single soul literally anywhere to be seen...

"Can this be real?!" I say to myself. "Can I be the only person in the centre of the city between Placa Cataluna all down La Rambla and down to the harbourside? On a Saturday afternoon at 16.10pm?!"

I again make a mental note: this is insane...am I dreaming...this may never ever happen again in this city....has it ever happened before now? Then "I'm the one standing here", I unconsciously mutter under my breath in complete and utter disbelief. The realisation of what I have just thought is mind-blowing. I have the centre of the city to myself, WOW!!

.... And with '28 Days Later' firmly in my mind, I walk amazed, back to the buzzer on her apartment door, entering as if nothing just happened and we are together in our aloneness, in this city of sleeping angels.

A Happy Ending
by Ann

Ann is a sixty-something retired educationalist, determined to grow old disgracefully, pandemic or no pandemic! She moved to Edinburgh during the pandemic and is grateful to have survived and lived to tell the tale.

2019 ended on a high note. It had been a good year, a happy year. I spent October and November at my place in Florida and in December went on holiday with friends to Krakow. We did visit Auschwitz, maintaining almost complete silence during 'the tour', as it seemed deeply disrespectful to the millions who had suffered and died, to make banal conversation.

Later in December, I travelled to Edinburgh to spend Christmas with my daughter and son-in-law, and his parents. This was a special Christmas, as it was the time I finally made the decision to move from Cheshire to Scotland. It had been on the cards for a long time, so it was with much excitement I returned home at the end of December to plan my move.

Headaches have been an unwelcome but not particularly serious feature of my life for years, so even when this headache in mid-January seemed to last a bit longer than normal, I wasn't too worried. Then, the projectile vomiting started, alongside what I now know is termed 'brain fog', together with a level of debilitating exhaustion I had never before experienced. My throat was so sore, but medicated throat sweets had no effect at all. A persistent cough and shortness of breath finally convinced me to seek help.

A call to 111, led to an urgent appointment with a GP, which in turn led to a trip to A&E. After a chest X-ray, blood tests and several hours collapsed on a plastic chair outside the Assessment Unit, a doctor informed me I was being admitted. Apparently, my temperature was sky high and my blood pressure very low. Her diagnosis was, "we're not sure what's wrong but you can't go home."

The hospital was full to bursting – there were simply no beds available, so I was given a bed in the Assessment Unit, where I was hooked up to a drip dispensing antibiotics and painkillers, whilst various tablets were offered to stem the nausea.

Three days later I overheard a conversation between two nurses. It seemed the Ward Doctor had been instructed to discharge three patients from the unit because several people had been waiting all night to be admitted. So, I was discharged, even though no one had explained what was causing my illness. My discharge letter read: "Reason for admission: Generally unwell". "Diagnosis: Infection? Source?" That was it. I was given a box of antibiotics and home I went.

The next three months are somewhat of a blur. My energy levels were at rock bottom and the brain fog was so severe that, at my lowest point, I contemplated whether this was actually the onset of dementia. The realisation that I had almost certainly been suffering from COVID-19 came slowly, as the media began reporting the emerging list of symptoms.

Three courses of antibiotics, one intravenous and two oral, had proved ineffective. The sore throat continued for months, untouched by the antibiotics, painkillers and special syrup prescribed by my GP. In February 2020 I had developed conjunctivitis. The fever disappeared, so I guess the medication had done some good.

Looking back on the conversations I had with my daughter whilst I was in hospital, I had asked, "How can the hospital kitchen make a cheese sandwich taste like lard and vinegar?" The following day I remarked, "I expected the cheese bake to be bland but how can they take all the flavour out of potatoes??" Change of taste and loss of taste are, as we now know, key symptoms of COVID-19.

By April 2020, I finally summoned the energy to begin the process of moving to Scotland. A family friend, who is a builder, fixed everything that needed to be fixed in my house and in July the house went on the market. A few friends thought I was quite mad! Questions were voiced, such as "Why don't you wait until the pandemic is over?" "How are you going to move in the middle of a lockdown?" and "Are you sure it's a good idea to have random people tramping around your house?" They gave me food for thought but my mind was made up. Given the duration of the pandemic, which is still with us in March 2022, I'm glad I didn't wait for it to be over!

The house sold in July 2020, to the first person who had viewed it. They would be cash buyers on the sale of their home and I had decided to move initially into rented accommodation. Unfortunately, we ended up in a chain of five buyers and sellers, and the whole process took six and a half months! Estate agents, solicitors and council staff were all working from home. Post went astray, a buyer dropped out and two days before exchange we were told that the Help to Buy funds hadn't come through for the buyer at the bottom of the chain.

There were times when I did wonder whether this move was ever going to happen, but in January 2021 I delivered my keys to the agent. I jumped in the car and drove two hundred and twenty miles in a thunderstorm and gale force winds to Edinburgh.

Pandemic or no pandemic, my new life was to begin.

My own illness, together with planning my move to Scotland dominated much of my time during 2020. I was privileged to spend a lot of time walking in the fresh air, often alone but sometimes with friends, and I had a lovely garden where I could relax. I was acutely aware that many, many people (indeed including my daughter and son-in-law) lived in flats with no outside space and I wondered how they were coping. I chose to be extremely careful and limited my contact with the outside world, giving up my beloved badminton and swimming. I knew I might have compromised immunity due to a genetic kidney condition, so taking unnecessary risks would have been reckless. Physically I finally recovered from COVID-19 and I thankfully remained mentally strong.

The fragility of human life and the responsibility to make the most of every day was brought into sharp focus with the news that a close friend had been diagnosed with pancreatic cancer. I was, and remain, in awe of her strength and resolve.

In early 2021, a few weeks after I moved, my sister too became unwell. Doctors variously diagnosed heart failure and/or Long Covid. GPs were obviously under immense pressure and arranging home visits was a challenge. Physical distance creates its own difficulties and this was exacerbated by on-going travel restrictions. I have managed to visit her and I'm desperately concerned, though she does seem to be getting a little stronger over time. 2020 and 2021 were the worst possible years to fall ill. My friend and my sister have made it, against all the odds, for which I am eternally grateful.

Notwithstanding illness and anxieties, 2021 was also a very happy year. It was the first time for over a decade that my daughter, son-in-law and I have lived in the same city and we have rejoiced in the ability to 'pop over' to see one another every week. Restaurants, cinemas, theatres and gyms are no longer places to be avoided, though I still wear a face covering in all public places. I have bought my new home in Edinburgh and begun to make a life and new friends here. With the whole family and seemingly all of my friends, triple jabbed, I can only hope that this living nightmare is coming to an end.

Too many families have lost loved ones. My thoughts are with them.

Locked Down at Everest Base Camp
by Alyssa

Alyssa is an avid traveller. She has worked on all kinds of projects around the world and now teaches in the Lake Tahoe area of California. Read her travel blog at: www.takingthelongway.com

(There are some American spellings in this chapter.)

I first heard about the novel COVID-19 while visiting Namibia. It was mid-February 2020, and my partner and I were sitting on a sun-dappled terrace one golden afternoon. Gary was scanning through his WhatsApp messages as I sipped on a stein of beer, gazing out at the Atlantic. He cleared his throat before reading a text from his uncle aloud. "Stevie is saying there's this new virus called COVID-19, seems to think it might actually be serious." Gary paused, squinting into the brightness of the day before putting on his sunglasses. "Think we should be worried?" he asked, tracing the frosty rim of his glass as he spoke. Here in the idyllic German expat town of Swakopmund, whatever might be happening in Wuhan felt impossibly far away. "Nah… probably just a slow news cycle," I yawned. "Should we go for a swim?"

Gary and I had been working together as seasonal outdoor educators for years. Typically, we worked four or five months in the United States while living out of a Toyota Highlander, and then worked four or five months overseas while living out of two 60-liter backpacks. Our time on the clock was spent taking students hiking, camping, kayaking and climbing, and our priorities during our months off were the same. Early in 2020 we had attended a friend's wedding in South Africa, before road tripping our way up the coast through Namibia. Work would be starting in just a few days, with our schedule for the upcoming year jam-packed between gigs in Borneo, mainland Malaysia, Bali and South Korea.

Landing in Singapore from southern Africa, we noticed immediately that the normal buzz of the city had been reduced to a subdued hum. Singapore consistently served as our hub for the region, with its efficiency, cleanliness, and safety – achieved through a slight authoritarian bent – always appreciated after weeks out in the woods. This visit, nearly everyone we encountered was wearing face coverings. Temperature checks were required to enter the city's many corridors of malls, where we purchased a packet of masks out of what felt like an abundance of caution. After spending a couple of days recovering from jetlag and adjusting to the humidity, we caught a flight to Borneo. Emerging from two weeks in the Malay jungle, we connected to Wifi to find out that all of our work for March had been cancelled.

Our company flew us to Kuala Lumpur, where we booked a last-minute Airbnb. Over a hurried phone call, our boss assured me from Korea that work would be back by April. "Think of it as a vacation! Just enjoy the month. We aren't worried, I'll plan on seeing you April 3rd." Following a brief discussion and a quick AirAsia search, we purchased two round trip tickets to Nepal, shocked by our impulsivity. As an avid hiker, the Three Passes Trek through the Everest region had been at the top of my bucket list for years. We would disappear into the mountains, confident that when we re-emerged in a month, life would return to normal.

A temperature scan was the only difference in normal airport protocol upon arrival in Kathmandu. As we taxied into the chaos of the capital, honking horns, ringing bells, crowing roosters, barking dogs and revving engines created a constant roar of sound. Colorful prayer flags and lines of laundry extended across the rooftops of crumbling buildings, criss-crossing narrow alleyways. Motorbikes driven by women in beautiful saris wove between cars and around rickshaws, while two cows stood petulantly in the middle of a busy intersection. A bus screeched around them with a honk, "Buddha Was Born in Nepal" printed across its bumper.

The next two days were spent fighting sensory overload as we rented cold weather gear and explored the touristy, bustling Thamel neighborhood. At 4am we hoisted our fully loaded backpacks on top of a Jeep bound for Salleri, and eleven queasy hours later, we finally reached the foothills of the Himalayas. In our first days hiking we strolled through vivid green rice terraces, encountering few other tourists. We passed by forests of blooming rhododendron trees and gazed out at sweeping vistas, thrilled at our first glimpse of snowy mountaintops.

Despite its reputation as the most dangerous airport in the world, most tourists still opt to fly into Lukla. As soon as we reached the airport the trail grew crowded with trekkers suffering from the abrupt change in altitude. Weaving around donkeys loaded with backpacks and mobs of people, was not my normal idea of a good time in nature. While to me it felt congested, over lunch a guide worriedly explained that the current number of visitors was only about 5% of the normal amount. Continuing upwards we watched the scenery gradually change, swirling mist obscuring the increasingly steep hillsides. After one final push we arrived in Namche Bazaar, the unofficial capital of the Himalayas. Situated in a bowl-shaped valley carved precariously into a hillside, the town's many bars, restaurants, gear shops and bakeries contrasted strangely with the pristine 6,000-meter peaks surrounding it.

Like so many before us, from this point onwards we were completely enthralled by the rugged beauty of the Himalayas. During our acclimatization day in Namche, we had joined up with a couple heading in the same direction, Joy and Tom from Canada and England, respectively. Fir trees perfumed the air, and instead of donkeys we now tiptoed past groups of slow, gentle-eyed yaks. As we eased into the trek, a rhythm developed: each morning we would wake up at a different tea house and enjoy breakfast together. Then, we would repeatedly lose elevation, use a rickety suspension bridge to cross a river, and wind slowly uphill on the other side to climb even higher. Afternoons on trail were spent panting as we leap-frogged past one another, offering weary high fives at each new bend.

Even with the extreme altitudes, freezing temperatures and physical strain, I was still living in a blissed-out bubble, with each day more spectacular than the last. I marvelled at the different angles of Ama Dablam, and stopped to explore colorful, pastel-painted monasteries. While checking into a guesthouse I would be asked questions like "Would you like a valley view with the sunset, or an Everest view with the sunrise?" Evenings were spent sharing pots of tea on the rooftop with little groups of tourists from all over the world, the sunset painting layers of snowy mountains cotton candy pink. At dawn the chanting of monks served as our alarm clock. Throughout the day I would catch myself smiling contentedly, humbled by the vastness all around me.

Without much preparation I had managed to haul myself to the bottom of Kongma La, our first major pass. I was feeling reasonably confident that I could complete the following day's ten kilometer journey, heading up to 5,540 meters and then back down and across a glacier, especially since the idea of a rest day in Lobuche was proving incredibly motivating. The next morning our party of four sipped our soup in the early morning darkness, before stepping outside and immediately sinking knee-deep into fresh powder. Overnight we had received an unexpected dump of snow that completely obscured the cairns marking the trail. For now we could follow the footprints of an earlier group, so we set off, hoping that their lead would get us across the pass.

Within the first hour the air began to feel so thin that I was only able to take one step for each full breath. For every gain uphill I also slid back a half step, as I white-knuckled my trekking poles, attempting to stay in place. Six hours later, I finally clawed my way to the top of the pass. With Lobuche now in sight I felt relieved, even as my water supply dwindled to only half a liter. Unfortunately, the party in front of us was still resting, so now our group was at the front breaking trail while also navigating blind. The fresh snow concealed a layer of oven-sized boulders, making each step a desperate guessing game to avoid sliding into the unseen crevices between rocks. By the time I reached the bottom my legs felt like two strands of cooked spaghetti. Overhead the clouds were threatening snow, so with no time to rest we continued on to cross the glacier.

Dehydrated and delirious, we finally stumbled in the front door of the tea house. It had taken us ten hours to walk ten kilometres. Too tired to attempt stairs, we collapsed onto sofas in the main room. Without prompting, the owner smiled and brought over large plates of pasta alongside mugs of hot lemon water. We ate in complete silence. After cleaning his plate, Tom looked up, sighing slowly. "I've hiked over 6,000 miles of trail, and today was the single most difficult day of my life." Everyone laughed, relieved to have made it. "Now I understand why people stop just 200 meters short of the summit of Everest," Joy chimed in, still chuckling. "Every step is the most exhausting thing you've ever done." Laughter hurt my wind-burned face, and unable to hold my head up any longer, I crawled into bed before seven.

I woke the next morning to find every inch of my body aching. With difficulty I forced myself out of my warm sleeping bag and tenderly limped downstairs. Propping myself up on a nest of pillows in the sunroom, I thawed out my toes while sleepily nursing a bright reddish-orange sea buckthorn juice. Joy had already finished breakfast and sat cross-legged, watercoloring a yak. Tom read a book as Gary played a half-hearted game of solitaire, the flutter of the cards and gentle scratching of Joy's paintbrush the only noise interrupting the silence. I had just started to doze off when the owner, Ema, who had been relaxing on a bench across from me, sat up with a gasp. Clutching her phone, she shook her mother awake, speaking in rapid-fire Nepali before turning to the rest of us, wide-eyed. "The government is saying that all tourists must leave. Now."

For a moment we all stared at one another, blinking dumbly. Then everyone leapt into motion at once, clamoring to find rupees and purchase overpriced Internet cards. One American ran upstairs to pack his bag, announcing loudly that he was calling a helicopter. In such a remote location, web pages loaded at a snail's pace, but eventually we realized it was true. Locals had forty-eight hours to choose a location to shelter in place, before cars would no longer be allowed on the road and no one would be permitted outside their homes. Tribhuvan International Airport would be closing its doors at 8pm the next day for an indeterminate amount of time. There was no further information. If we did not get to the capital and on a flight, we would be stuck in Nepal. I had woken up achy, but still feeling happy to be in such a remote place, disconnected from the world. Now, I felt frightened and too far away from everything — starting with the airport.

Even if we had the extra two thousand dollars the American was asking to share his helicopter, the odds of us reaching Lukla in time to vie for a space on one of the tiny propeller planes back to Kathmandu were not good. The return trek was over 50km of icy, strenuous hiking, and I still felt like I had lost a fight from the prior day's exertion. Tom and Joy stood in the doorway, reluctantly lacing their hiking boots. "We're going for it," Joy explained, heaving on her pack. "What's your plan?" Gary and I studied each other mutely, the realization crashing on us like a wave, slowly at first, then all at once. Eventually I replied. "We're staying."

After Tom and Joy left, we sat in a cramped corner near the stove, debating. In what can only be described as magical thinking, we concluded that since the country was shutting down, we might as well try to see Everest Base Camp. I hurriedly went to ask Ema, who had already started storing away the kitchen, if she could allow us to stay for one more night. She paused for a moment before nodding, smiling resolutely. I let out a sigh of relief before thanking her. "Dhanyabad, truly." The rest of the afternoon was spent with our phones glued to our hands, comparing updates with the few remaining guests while registering ourselves with the U.S. Embassy, and scanning Facebook expat groups for any news.

Our normal morning routine felt strangely empty without Tom and Joy, although our pattern stayed the same. Shiver out of bed and start packing, eat a breakfast of tea and ramen, then trudge slowly and painfully uphill for several hours. Gorak Shep was the only town so far that we found dingy and depressing, but the tea house fortunately remained open. Dropping our bags, we greeted some of the other panicked tourists desperately trying to refresh their screens, before continuing on to Base Camp.

This final push was not our longest distance or even our highest elevation, but every few steps I had to stop, leaning forward over my trekking poles to fight back the urge to vomit. Wheezing miserably, I eventually crested the hill for a bird's eye view of Base Camp. Since I was a child I had been borrowing my father's books about the Himalayas to study grainy photos taken from this exact spot, depictions of a buzzing tent city built adjacent to the iconic Khumbu Icefall. Instead, we were met with an eerie stillness. No colorful tents, no bustling mountaineers sorting their gear – in fact, the only evidence of humanity was 'Everest Base Camp' scrawled in spray paint across a sedan-sized boulder, and a few tattered prayer flags fluttering in the breeze. Walking closer, we fell into a stunned silence, craning our necks to take in the amphitheater of peaks surrounding us. Improbably, we were the only people at the foot of the tallest mountain in the world.

Clouds suddenly rolled in, obscuring the view and waking us from our reverie. As we walked down, a bitter headwind began to howl, stinging our faces. Back at the teahouse we huddled close to the stove for warmth. The yak dung used for fuel created an acrid smoke that caused our already struggling lungs to burn. A couple from the UK pulled up chairs alongside us, and through fits of coughing explained how they had quit their jobs, rented their house for the year, and booked an around the world ticket. "Nepal was our first stop," the woman went on, "and now we have nothing to go back to." As it neared eight o'clock, a strange countdown commenced, ticking down from ten. "3... 2... 1. Happy... Lockdown?" I tried to joke, my smile quickly turning to a grimace. As the fire waned, we all hobbled upstairs. Shivering, I climbed into my sleeping bag, watching little clouds of my own breath until I drifted off to sleep.

I awoke early the next morning with a start, drifts of snow swirling gently across my bed through a crack in the single pane window. Outside a blizzard raged, rendering everything a dizzying white. All night I had tossed and turned, gasping for air between bouts of nausea. Blowing on my hands to attempt to warm my frozen fingers, I began numbly stuffing my sleeping bag into its sack. My water bottle was completely frozen, as was the water in the squat toilet. I hadn't felt my feet in days, I was most likely hypoxic, and it had been weeks since I'd bathed – I was done.

This attitude might have proven problematic had our trip been continuing as normal, but we were now officially under lockdown. We still had received no additional information and had no idea exactly what was allowed. Rumors swirled that police were patrolling the mountains and arresting people found outside, or that every tea house was now deserted, stranding tourists in the storm. Still, staying where we were was not a viable option, so once the snow eased, we set off tentatively down the trail.

Just as we were passing the teahouse in Lobuche, Ema and her mother stepped outside to lock the door. The windows were now all tightly boarded, and they both carried giant backpacks with kettles and other cookware dangling off the bottoms. Before she waved goodbye, Ema cocked her head, worry evident on her face. "We live not so far from here, you know. If you are stuck, come to my village. You can help us farm potatoes until this passes." They were the first of many locals to outpace us that day as everyone hurriedly returned to their mother villages. Many wore flip flops or carried entire stoves strapped to their backs, still walking the rocky, icy paths with ease.

We descended sixteen kilometres before finding a tea house that had not been boarded up. Fortunately, the time passed quickly, as the oxygen grew thicker with every step and the temperatures finally warmed to a balmy zero degrees celsius. After a restless night and another long day hiking, we arrived at the picturesque village of Phortse. Scanning the town from above, we were surprised to spot a man running up the hillside towards us. He introduced himself while we nervously adjusted our packs, presenting us with a business card listing his many successful summits. "My name is Pemba. You're Alyssa and Gary, right? My niece, Ema, called to tell me to keep an eye out for you. I already prepared a room, just in case."

He led us through town to his tea house, where a plate of steaming momos was already laid out. Dazed by his kindness, we chatted with his family before connecting to the Wifi. Our hearts sank once we realized we still had not received any response from the Embassy. Uncertain if we would find another open tea house, and grateful for Pemba's hospitality, we decided to stay. The next three days were spent trying to speak to someone at the Tourism Board or the American Embassy, and reassuring our parents that we would eventually find a way home. In between we played a lot of cards, leaning our backs against a stone wall in the garden while tilting our faces towards the sun. The tension between resigned boredom and the adrenaline rush of sudden desperation gave me a stomach-ache. Still, the rest was much needed. I was able to shower with hot water from a bucket, practically a religious experience, and with a belly constantly full of momos and lemon ginger tea, I started to feel human again.

By day four our main source of information was coming from a "Tourists Stuck in Nepal" Facebook group, where it was becoming increasingly difficult to tell the difference between rumor and fact. Later that morning our phones finally lit up with a notification from the American Embassy. A terse email read, "Thank you for your patience. The embassy has arranged a chartered flight from Lukla at 8am tomorrow. Please arrive at the gate at 7am to receive your ticket." Worried about such a late start, we quickly said our goodbyes and began to hike the 27 kilometers to the airport. The previous sunny days quickly melted into relentless rain, turning the trail to slick mud. By the time we dragged our dirty, soggy bodies out of the mountains and into Lukla, it was nighttime and completely dark. All of the hostels were filled with other trapped tourists from around the world, and we grew increasingly desperate, eventually finding a dirty, windowless room to lay our heads for the night.

Early the next morning we were shocked to see the masses of people pressed against the fence surrounding the airport. The airport itself was not much larger than a football pitch, and we slowly pushed our way through the throng, listening for the loudest voices until we found the other Americans. At first everything seemed like complete chaos, but eventually we began to understand the system: Guards would yell out a nationality, and the crowd would surge forward, thrusting out passports until sixteen people had slipped inside; An hour or so later, those lucky sixteen would board a cartoonish propeller plane and roll down the frighteningly short 500 meter runway, dropping off a cliff at the end. Hungry and disoriented, the day was spent with our fellow citizens watching plane after plane take off, the American who had taken the helicopter from Lobuche studiously avoiding our gaze. Late in the afternoon we were turned away and told to return tomorrow.

The next day the process was the same, although this time our group was allowed inside the waiting room, only to have our flight canceled due to an incoming storm. We moved guesthouses to be directly next to the airport, and planned to arrive at 5am the following day. On the third morning we were the first group called. I drank an instant coffee in the waiting room, watching the airport staff repeatedly remove their masks to cough, before gleefully boarding our plane for a shaky flight to Kathmandu. An embassy representative met us at that airport, doing his best to answer our many questions, before herding us onto a shuttle bus. Everyone was then checked into an overpriced hotel and instructed not to leave the building for any reason. Once again, there was nothing to do but wait.

The next two days were spent obsessively refreshing my inbox. News arrived in drips: food shortages from border closures with India and China were imminent; the entire country of Nepal had only one ventilator. From the rooftop early one morning we watched police beat a man with their batons before carrying him away, a punishment for leaving his home. Later that afternoon, Gary still chose to collect our stored luggage and return our rental gear, furtively darting from building to building through Thamel. He returned unharmed but upset, describing how his footsteps echoed through the normally frenzied streets. "Everyone relies on tourism to make a living. What's going to happen to them?"

Another brief email appeared, with instructions to walk to the American Embassy Center on April 1st at 8am, and wait outside the gate wearing a face covering. Arriving at the pickup point, I was suddenly surrounded by more American accents than I had heard in months. As we waited in line, an embassy worker handed out soft pretzels, his cheeks pressed up towards his eyes. This was my first realization that even with a mask on you could tell when someone was smiling, and I made a mental note for my entry into this next phase of history. After a temperature check, I signed a waiver agreeing to repay the government, and then boarded a shuttle to take what would be my last flight for the foreseeable future.

The return journey felt surprisingly normal. People readjusted neck pillows, put in their headphones, or buzzed the flight attendants to order drinks. This familiarity was comforting, as I knew I would soon enter a world I no longer recognized. Seemingly overnight, everything had changed. For now, the plane remained a safe haven, shepherding me between the old and the new. I settled in with a sigh, heading home at last.

At 2am our plane touched down in Washington, D.C. Bleary-eyed, we shuffled through an unmanned health station, thermometers and questionnaires strewn haphazardly across the tables. A group of Mormon missionaries from another flight, clean cut and chipper, queued in the immigration line in front of me. Popping my American SIM card back into my phone, the first text I received was from my friend Anthony. "Trump says 100,000 dead will be a win. Stay safe."

The next morning we walked to the central train station. In my junior year of university I had lived in D.C. for an internship, and the lack of traffic or pedestrians during what would normally be rush hour was disconcerting. We bought our tickets to New York from an automated machine, a lone, homeless woman's babble echoing off the cavernous main hall. Four hours later our train pulled into the New Rochelle station. Gary's parents had come to pick us up in two separate cars, and we chatted from a distance before Eliot and Louise drove back together, and we loaded our bags into the other vehicle. As soon as we parked at their house we took the stairs down to the basement, where we would quarantine for the next two weeks.

By the time we resurfaced, we had recovered from our jet lag and Khumbu coughs. For the next month we waited at

Gary's childhood home, clinging to the idea that all of this was temporary, and life would soon return to normal. By the end of the first week we had reverted to teenagers, staying up to watch terrible television, giggling as we raided the fridge and microwaved late night quesadillas. Louise, a former Broadway star, kept the kitchen stocked with warm cookies, humming show tunes as she baked. For breakfast, bagels and cream cheese seemed to appear like magic. I couldn't remember the last time I'd had so little responsibility. The days were spent doing one thousand piece puzzles and playing board games. Eliot spent nearly all his time in the backyard gardening, while I opted for long meandering strolls around the neighborhood to watch spring unfold, crossing the street whenever I spotted another person. When I came upstairs one morning to find Gary opening a new puzzle, a beer in one hand and a cookie in the other, I realized it was time to move on.

My uncle graciously offered us his cabin in a small mountain town in Northern California, while he was gone for the summer fighting wildfires. After a joyless drive out west, every day was spent frantically applying for jobs in places we thought we might want to live. An introvert, I was surprised by how much I missed the casual daily interactions that I had always taken for granted. On weekly visits to the supermarket I'd fumble through the complicated check out process, focused on sanitizing in the correct order instead of complimenting the clerk on her fuchsia sweater. Casual hugs or handshakes became a thing of the past, as I adjusted to caring for people by staying away from them. Terms like "herd immunity" became a part of my daily lexicon, where every conversation inevitably circled back to the pandemic. What I missed the most was the feeling of stability. I began to mourn our collective loss of certainty.

Without a job or a community, I found myself suffering from a strange loss of self. I had not realized previously how much of my identity was tied to my nomadic lifestyle. Rethinking my entire life grew increasingly challenging once the initial months of national unity began to dissipate. COVID-19 denial began running rampant throughout the country. Black Lives Matter protests erupted across the nation, followed shortly by historic wildfires along the West Coast. To me it felt as though the country's communal grief was now tangible, visible in the black skies overhead, in the ash I wiped off my car each morning.

Eventually I accepted a job in a different California mountain town, running a COVID-19 clinic and contact tracing. Over breakfast I would scan the news, reading about anti-mask protests across the state. As I pulled on my PPE in an elaborate daily ritual I would listen to podcasts, hearing stories about people in hospitals dying alone, using their last breath to protest that it wasn't COVID-19. Contact tracing often caused me to wonder if humanity was worthy of continued hope. Afternoons were spent on the phone with angry members of my community, asking them to stay home from school or work. Many refused to get tested or to wear a mask. I tried to stay professional, while also conveying that we could not simply normalize death because we longed for a return to normal and that we had an obligation to care about one another.

My life of constant movement and adventure had shifted so dramatically that the past started to feel like some sort of fantastical dream. Despondency led to a creative block, then a general numbness. Time shifted and warped, seemingly standing still from April of 2020. I blinked and it was somehow June of 2021 before I felt like myself again, stepping out into the summer sunshine groggy and dazed.

While reflecting after writing this story on the second anniversary of the lockdown, it became clear to me that this moment in history has served as a great unveiling. We can no longer deny how deeply interconnected we all are. Whether fighting against racism, climate change, or a deadly virus, a few simply cannot save the whole. If we do not learn to prioritize the well-being of our most vulnerable communities, we will be lost. As we continue living through a global pandemic, I do not think that we should feel any obligation to find beauty or goodness in suffering. Still, part of me believes that our grief is slowly carving out a path to eventually allow for more deeply felt bliss. In my life I can see this alchemy already, beginning with the gratitude I now have for the small pleasures of being human. Whether savoring the aroma of my morning coffee, gazing at the blue skies overhead, or delighting in the laughter of loved ones, an insistence on joy and an insistence on hope are necessary muscles for surviving these difficult times. We must continue to seek out sweetness, or risk losing sight of what is worth saving.

Gratitudes
by Maud

Maud (not her real name) is an ex-teacher from London. In 1991, she set up a children's day nursery in Devon, with her husband and by 2019 was looking forward to a retirement in France. She has three grown-up children and four grandchildren.

Part One

My COVID-19 story really began in the summer of 2019. My husband and I felt it was time to step back from the nursery business we'd been running for over 28 years – "now or never", we felt. So, we booked a short August holiday in Brittany, whilst we looked around for somewhere to live during the autumn months. We wanted a base and time to look around France for a house to buy. Although the Brexiteers had won the referendum, we were still hopeful that delays would mean it might never actually happen. We'd already sold our house and were renting, then living with our daughter, son-in-law and their three young boys, in Plymouth.

By September, we'd moved into an amazing gite near Auray, and enjoyed weeks of sun, solitude, walks on beaches and in the forest. It also transpired to be the wettest autumn in years, so we endured incessant rain and mud. We were regularly invited for meals with the gite owners, who became good friends, taking us to the local market and giving us crates of their home-made cider. By December 2019, we'd found a 'longere' in the Vendeé, signed the 'compromis' and taken a road trip to Barcelona to spend Christmas with our sons.

By January 2020, we were hearing talk of a 'virus' that was spreading around the world, but we took little notice of the 'rumour-mongers' and laughed it off – some people were being alarmist (as usual), we thought. Life for us carried on as planned, so in February, we brought our two eldest grandchildren to spend the half term holiday with us in the gite, while still waiting for all the paperwork to go through on the house purchase. Out of the blue, and as we ordered cakes and coffee in the supermarket café in Auray, I had the second massive attack that was to change my life – not COVID-19 related, but I'll explain later.

Our moving-in date was set for March 9th 2020. So after that February half term, we returned to Plymouth with the grandchildren, hired a van, packed up as much of our belongings as we could fit in, got the Roscoff ferry back to France and drove down to the Vendeé. The arrangement was that after we had dropped off everything at the house and returned the van to the UK (which we did on March 11th), we'd call back at the gite the following week to collect the remainder of our things. So far, so normal.

Our return crossing to France was booked for the night of March 17th 2020 (St. Patrick's Day). Unfortunately, over the weekend before, I had developed a raging temperature and sore throat. We jokingly said, "hope it's not that Coronavirus!", but I wasn't having trouble breathing. Over the phone, the GP prescribed antibiotics and paracetamol and said it was a throat infection. I was told on no account to actually go to the surgery. Initially, I was determined to get the night ferry on March 17th as planned, but by that morning, feeling no better and with my temperature still high, I caved in and the trip was cancelled. Amazingly, although we had virtually given them no notice, Brittany Ferries refunded our ticket. They had already started putting out information about people not travelling if they felt ill, had a temperature or a sore throat. Still, we joked about me having "Coronavirus" – and whether I did or not, became irrelevant in the scheme of things.

By the next day, I was getting emails from our nursery parents asking if we were planning to stay open. At that point, sitting up in bed in my daughter's house in Plymouth and still feeling unwell, I replied, "We are staying open unless directed to close" and posted updates on our Facebook page. As a staff team, we were having heated debates as to whether we could close by choice – or whether we needed to be forced to close by the Government. We needed to know where we would stand with parents – not only those receiving Early Years funding from the Local Authority, but those paying fees. We had no idea what would happen about paying staff if we were closed and had no income. The words 'unprecedented times' were to be repeated over and over again. Sitting in our daughter's kitchen, we compared it with what it must have been like before World War 2 was announced - with us huddled close to our TVs, as people then huddled close to their radios.

Still feeling quite shaky and exhausted, I was well enough by Friday, March 20th, 2020, to email all our parents. I explained that in the early hours of that morning, the Government had issued clarification on the closure of schools and early years settings such as ours, but said that we would remain open. However, only children who needed specialist support, or were 'vulnerable', or had a parent working in one of the critical sectors (which we listed), could continue to attend the nursery. Therefore we hastily checked our lists of children with additional needs and asked every parent to let us know whether or not their job was deemed to be "critical to the COVID-19 response".

We told parents it was paramount that we did everything we could to prevent the virus from spreading and this included keeping children at home if at all possible, even if parents were critical workers. We implored parents to be vigilant, to keep their child at home if they seemed unwell and that they would need to collect their child from nursery if their child developed a persistent cough, or had a temperature above 37.8°C. We were very clear that if their child, or anyone in their household had any of the COVID-19 symptoms, they could not return to nursery for fourteen days. We urged parents not to rely for childcare on anyone with 'underlying health conditions', whether they be grandparents, friends, or family members and that they should do everything they could to ensure children were not mixing socially in a way that would continue to spread the virus. We shared our enhanced cleaning and 'fogging' procedures, tried to group children in 'bubbles' and spread the word about thorough and regular hand washing.

However, that was only half the story. In March 2020, we had two nurseries and employed sixteen staff. Therefore I spent whole days trawling through precise Government guidelines, having conversations with ACAS and within our team, because if we had fewer children attending as a result of the COVID-19 outbreak, we would clearly not have enough work for everyone. So I had written to all the staff offering three 'Options':- work reduced hours (Option 1) , make redundancies (Option 2), or take paid/unpaid leave (Option 3). 'Stressful' would be an understatement. Then the word 'furlough' entered our vocabulary.

On March 26th, 2020, I emailed staff again, this time informing them of 'Option 4'. The Chancellor (Rishi Sunak) had announced a measure that took everyone by surprise - the Coronavirus Job Retention Scheme (CJRS). This enabled us to access financial support to continue paying part of our staff wages instead of making redundancies. To cut a long story short, staff could receive eighty percent of their pay and still accrue holiday, as long as they did not work!

Great, you would think. Problem solved. No, not really. Back to ACAS - I am an employer and this is a change in employment status. It is also a change that has the potential to cause division, because whilst our nursery remains open for keyworkers and vulnerable children, some staff are clearly being paid not to work, whilst others are working for their pay. So we consulted with our team, asked for volunteers and set out a 'priority' list (in case we had too many volunteers!) and prepared a Contractual Agreement which set out the new terms and conditions of employment. Thankfully, it all worked very well. The smaller of our nurseries closed, because the majority of parents either weren't eligible or were themselves 'furloughed'. Those parents who needed childcare were offered places at our larger nursery – and one member of staff offered to move across, so that there would be some continuity for those children.

In many ways, the period between March and the end of May 2020, was amazing. We were in almost daily contact with parents and posted many updates on our Facebook page. We kept parents informed of activities we were doing with those children who were able to attend, with lots of photos. We invited parents of children who were not able to attend, to send in photos of what they were doing at home and we posted weekly videos of staff engaging in a variety of 'learning' activities. We mastered the daily register that we had to submit to the Local Authority and made telephone contact with the families of 'vulnerable' children who weren't attending. We slightly reduced our opening and closing times to allow for the enhanced washing and disinfecting of the resources used during the day, of table-tops and door handles, bannisters and lunchboxes. Parents were understanding and no-one complained. Of the staff who opted to remain at work, none were off sick and none took time off, so we felt a real team. We kept in regular contact with those staff who were furloughed. Again, we made reference amongst ourselves to the sense of community we imagined people must have felt during the war and every day, we tuned in to listen to Johnson and his team at 5pm. Later, we went out on our doorsteps at home to 'clap' for the NHS – and wave to our neighbours! However, it's hard to imagine just how anxious we were about keeping our distance, about leaving the house only for "essential" reasons (and for having "proof" should we be stopped by the police). I will never forget the sight of long, snaking queues of individual masked people, with their individual trolleys waiting to be let into the supermarket! Luckily, we were a household 'bubble', so didn't experience the terrible loneliness and fear of people who had to isolate alone.

Eventually, armed with a mountain of paperwork, my husband and I virtually held our breath as we drove from Plymouth to Kent, to get the train to Calais. No hotels would accept anyone except keyworkers, so we spent a night in my sister and brother-in-law's garden summer house, before driving to Folkestone. The roads were empty. It was very strange. At any moment, we expected to be stopped by the "COVID-19 police". Arriving successfully in France, we drove to our gîte and were only stopped once. As we started to get out our papers (showing we owned a house in France), they waved us on our way.

From our house in the Vendeé countryside, we continued to email parents and spoke to staff on a daily basis. By the end of May 2020, the Government was allowing settings to open up once again. So I spent hours writing up and explaining our COVID-19 policies, the procedures to be followed to keep everyone safe and how we were going to stagger the return of children and staff from June 1st. But life was much the same in France as in England. Shops, workplaces, entertainment venues were all closed. Only one person from your household could go to the supermarket at a time. Mask wearing and social distancing was compulsory and all trolleys were disinfected before and after use. There was a palpable eeriness about daily life.

However, as the summer wore on, things changed. In August 2020, we travelled to Ireland for a family wedding; we permanently closed our smaller nursery and we travelled back and forth to France as we took more of our stuff over to the new house and children came to stay. At the end of August 2020, my husband and I were back in Plymouth once again. Then everything changed for us on Sept 5th.

Part Two

Flashback to September 2019. This is when the second part of my COVID-19 'story' began – on September 28th to be precise. We'd settled into the gitê in Brittany earlier in the month, but I had returned to attend a conference in

London with my daughter, Lauren (not her real name). There had been a nice little buffet, but because of road works on the M4, our journey home was delayed and we were hungry. We stopped at Gordano Services at about 9pm and I ordered fish & chips. Lauren ordered something much healthier!

By the time we reached Plymouth it was nearly midnight and weirdly, I had a sort of 'hunger pains' feeling, so made a cup of hot chocolate to take to bed. Before I could even sip it, I began to feel terrible. The pain quickly became severe, quite high up in my chest and I began vomiting savagely. Sweat was literally running down my face. I had to strip off – stark naked, hanging over the toilet bowl.

Eventually, it began to ease off. It was past 1am, everyone was asleep and I sat crying on the toilet floor in self-pity and fear – because no one had heard me and I thought I was dying. Slowly, I crept up to bed and in the morning had two blood-shot eyes and felt exhausted. I put it down to food poisoning.

That was September 2019. Fast forward to that February half term in 2020, where it happened for the second time, in the supermarket toilet in France. I'd ordered coffee, cakes and juice for everyone, but had that 'hunger pain' feeling and just knew what was coming. Oh my God, it was terrible. I didn't want to call my husband because I didn't want to scare the boys. Locked in the toilet, once again I had to strip naked because the sweat was so bad.

Every now and then someone would try to get in and I'd shout "occupe". Then my husband banged on the door and said they were calling the supervisor, but I said just to wait. It had already begun to ease off. I didn't want to go to the hospital. I just wanted to go back to the gite and sleep.

When we returned to Plymouth after that February holiday with the boys, I had a minor recurrence one evening, just as we were about to tuck into a Chinese meal. So this time I made a doctor's appointment and was quickly sent to the hospital for a scan. The result was that I had gallstones. So, not too bad, I thought. They could be controlled by diet. I wasn't happy, but I wasn't worried.

To re-cap on events, shortly after this episode, we had returned to France, completed our house purchase (on March 9th), got back to Plymouth with the van and I'd been ill with that 'throat infection'. By mid-March, the COVID-19 'lockdown' was in full swing, but by May 2020 we were back in France. We then yo-yoed back and forth between Plymouth and France over the summer of 2020.

Back in Plymouth again the week after the August Bank Holiday 2020, tying up loose ends for what was definitely going to be the 'Big Move', **it** happened again. This time, I said to my husband, "take me to A& E, I can't take this anymore!" It was September 5th, 2020.

I was admitted to hospital that night with suspected pancreatitis (having had a COVID-19 swab test a few hours earlier). However, in the early hours of the morning, a doctor came and said that a gallstone had probably "gone walkabout" and that I'd be going down to the operating theatre shortly. Strangely enough, I felt a bit better by then (perhaps because of the drugs I'd been given) and seriously began to wonder if I'd been making a huge fuss about nothing. However, I didn't go down to theatre that morning. Instead, I went for several different scans over the course of the following days – and had two more COVID-19 swab tests. At one point there was a lot of scurrying around and beeps going off, then word went round the ward that someone had "tested positive"! We weren't supposed to know, so that felt quite scary.

On the afternoon of September 10th, 2020, a different doctor arrived with a nurse I hadn't seen before. They pulled the blue curtains round my bed and the doctor introduced herself. Then she said the nurse was a cancer support specialist. That didn't register at all. Then the doctor said that unfortunately the scans had shown several tumours and that I had pancreatic cancer. I heard the words, but I was very calm. I asked if she was sure because I knew I had gallstones (passive-aggressively perhaps suggesting she didn't know what she was talking about!). She said that there would be more scans and that the cancer nurse would be on hand to support me, but yes, she was sure. I remember smiling and saying, "this doesn't sound possible".

The moment they left, I burst into silent crying. No way. Not me. Not now. The curtains parted and a woman from the bed opposite came in quietly. She gave me a hug and actually said, "sod social distancing. I know neither of us have COVID!" I remember laughing at that even while I was crying.

About an hour later I walked down the ward to have a shower. I needed to think. I needed to start planning things for when I wouldn't be around. I needed to decide if I would tell anyone – or not – and if I did, how I would say it. Would I just be matter-of-fact, or would it be 'end of days'? Visitors were not being allowed onto the ward, so I'd only spoken to my family (and the staff at nursery), on the phone during the week. Could I just drop it into the conversation, or wait till I was discharged? Everything around me was very normal, but hundreds of thoughts were going round in my head. In the shower I started crying again – and understood the term 'silent scream'. My over-riding thoughts were, "not me, not now".

Later, I rang my husband and told him over the phone, but played it down, saying I needed to have a few more scans, but that this was what they were thinking. My daughter had been at the hospital for an appointment and rang me to say she had some things for me. I said to tell the ward reception to let me know when she was at the door, as I needed to speak to her. Although no visitors could come onto the ward, I was able to go outside in the corridor, both of us masked up. As soon as she approached me she knew something was wrong. We were very brave. We hugged. We didn't cry. She said that this was what she'd been worried about six months earlier when they'd diagnosed gallstones. The next day I was discharged from hospital.

By the time I'd got to their house, Lauren and my son-in-law had already been to Holland & Barrett and bought an array of vitamins and supplements, which were 'good' for people with cancer. In less than three weeks, I'd had a PET scan and a week after that, I'd had a 'telephone appointment' with my consultant. Everything I read and one or two people I spoke to, knew that pancreatic cancer was a real killer. Early diagnosis and treatment would be crucial – three months from one to the other seemed the magic number. Phone calls and conversations I had with my cancer nurse over those weeks have become a bit of a blur.

One reason for that is because two weeks after my diagnosis, my daughter had confirmation she had cervical cancer. She would require a radical hysterectomy with all the risks that involved. I had accused her of being a 'girl in a hurry' when she'd become pregnant at the age of twenty-two. By the time she was thirty, thank God she had three lively and healthy boys. Although she hadn't wanted more children, by 2020 the choice was being taken away from her.

Initially, we didn't tell our sons (Lauren's older brothers). One was working in Spain and we didn't want him to be on his own when he heard the news. Spain had gone into tight lockdown at the beginning of 2020 and he'd found that very hard. Our other son had just started a one-year PGCE, so we didn't want to tell him until he was a few weeks into the course. As it happens, our son in Spain lost his job because of the pandemic and was able to return home a few weeks later. At the same time, schools were being massively impacted, so our younger son had to rapidly take on the digital world of remote learning - 'Zoom', 'Teams' and 'OneNote'. If one thing is for sure as a result of the pandemic, it's that our vocabulary has now expanded.

Unlike the first few months of the pandemic, these months were an anxious time. Twice, we both had operation dates cancelled because intensive care beds or surgeons weren't available. Each time COVID-19 swabs had to be taken beforehand and we had to self-isolate – very difficult if living within a family home! However, considering what was happening all around the world and the life-threatening delays to major surgery for so many people, we were very lucky. I had my operation on November 17th and Lauren had hers on December 2nd, 2020.

The level of fear around contracting COVID-19 was intense and persisted into the spring of 2021. Once I realised that we would have to be in Plymouth for the long haul, my husband and I had started renting a house in November 2020. So by the time I was discharged from hospital, we had serious 'rules' in place! Anyone entering the house had to remove shoes and coats at the door then go straight to wash their hands. No one used 'my' towel. We actually had two large plastic boxes in the house so that when my husband came in, for example, from shopping or from the nursery, he would take off his clothes down to his boxers and put them in one box. Then he would wash his hands and put on the 'clean' clothes that were in the other box. Luckily, one of the bedrooms had an en-suite bathroom. Obviously, I claimed that for me, so no-one shared my bathroom or toilet - and anyone with the slightest sniffle was sent to have a COVID-19 test!

As 2021 wore on, we embraced 'positivity' and 'abundance' and we said our 'gratitudes' every day. We 'meditated' with Deepak Chopra. We went for long walks on Dartmoor, took up Cold Water Swimming and bought our DryRobes – Lauren and me, that is, not my husband! Despite some setbacks, both our operations have been successful.

But, as we move into 2022, it's not over yet. At the time of writing, (March 2022) it's still compulsory to wear a mask in shops and restaurants in France. To have any 'sit-down' food or drink, to go to the swimming pool or any place of entertainment, access is only allowed if you can show your 'Pass Sanitaire' (evidence that you've had all three vaccines). Travelling abroad has become complicated and extortionately expensive when the costs of PCR tests over the last two years have been added. So our dream of moving to start a new life in France, punctuated by the frequent visits of family and friends, is at the whim of governments.

I probably feel more vulnerable than I did before all this, as I try not to 'catch' anything. I need daily medication and regular check-ups and, as a result of my initial operation, I'm now waiting for a hernia repair. I also have Type 3C diabetes. As a result of her operation, Lauren is also waiting for further surgery. Life has changed for us, not all of it due to the pandemic.

Footnote

By June 2022, travel between France and the UK has become much easier for 'fully vaccinated' people as PCR tests, 'compelling' reasons for travel and 'sworn statements', are no longer necessary. Ironically, most members of my extended family and most of our employees, have now had COVID-19. Only yesterday, my son tested positive!

Under Pressure: Learning to Be Me.

by Tracey

Tracey is founder and principal of *Artinforms,* and co-founder of *Conscious Drumming.* She is a practising visual artist, musician, author, researcher, and natural wellness specialist. Along with her husband and wee dog, she lives in rural Aotearoa, New Zealand, and loves to draw her inspiration and energy from Nature.

Lockdown!

Mandatory isolation.

Imprisonment in my own home!

Must stay within my own boundaries.

Hmmm, such alarming words! And yet, perhaps it sounds like a perfect time to focus deep instead of spreading so wide? I have a long habit of getting too busy and spread too thin.

The beginning of New Zealand's 2020 lockdowns came a week before my husband and I were set to travel to Canada to visit family, especially our elderly mothers. Naturally, I felt huge disappointment. On the other hand, the situation was global and certainly beyond any personal effects, so I also felt a certain peace with it, and we settled in to 'make do' along with everyone else.

Going out for basics such as grocery shopping soon became traumatic events. Not only the fear of catching this new disease, but the compound fear of its unknown effect on those of us living with chronic conditions already. I have lived with multiple systemic conditions for over a decade. Since I already lived on the knife-edge of this delicate balancing act, I had learned a lot about what kept me healthy, or not. This new unknown virus was a particular worry due to CFS/Myalgic Encephalomyelitis (ME) often being described as a post-viral condition of the Epstein-Barr/mononucleosis/glandular fever viruses. What would the new virus do in this mix?

I am grateful to my husband for doing most of the shopping, and when home delivery services were scaled up to be available in our area, we made use of them regularly.

Staying home could then be received as a reward or relief, rather than an imposition. Isolation became a respite from the over-busy-ness I 'normally' felt while just trying to keep up the minimum activity in the world. Now I had time to rest, to read and research online. Now I could limit my interactions with other people, and all their attendant energies, to a few Zoom calls per day. My weeks actually became more manageable! I am highly sensitive to energy, so to have less interaction meant I could focus my own energy on areas of my own choosing, rather than just surviving the tides around me.

We were 'fortunate' to be living in a rural neighbourhood. It was a conscious choice to live where we did, so I don't call it luck, but I do recognize and am grateful for the position of choice. It made going for walks easy. We often only encountered two or three other people, if any. We felt strange to put a mask on and cross the street to avoid each others' airspace. But we all smiled and waved, everyone in the same boat: just trying to stay well - and sane!

I didn't suffer from 'withdrawal' of social contact that so many people were complaining of. I was enrolled that year in full time study. After a week or so off to reset their technology, our tutors did an outstanding job of continuing our classes remotely through Zoom. Certainly, it wasn't ideal, but we managed and in the end we all passed. However, our graduation ceremony was COVID-19-delayed three times and only just managed to happen eighteen months later. Slightly anticlimactic, but still worth it! We also started seeing friends and family by Zoom, one time even holding a games night.

So this was the good news, for which I'm eternally grateful. However, when the lockdowns finished, that was when my hell began.

I had felt somewhat weird that I was actually enjoying 'isolation' when so many were expressing feeling the trauma of missing out. What I didn't expect though, was the tidal wave of anxiety that swept into my life when it was time to go back out into the world. Because it was so unexpected and seemingly irrational, I took a long time to even fully identify what I was feeling. What was going on? Was it real and needing to be dealt with, or just a momentary "passing feeling"? Everyone was feeling some stress. I brushed it off, but it wouldn't step aside.

I felt like the ocean waves had suddenly swept the sand out from under my feet. I was off balance, struggling to stay afloat, and feeling fearful - fear of what I wasn't quite sure. This unexpected, overwhelming, and all-pervading sensation totally knocked my self-confidence out!

Looking back I can clearly recognize a trauma response had been triggered. But at the time, I couldn't quite believe it. Having spent decades training and healing myself, I thought I'd left all the 'out of control' feelings behind. For a long time I carried on, trying to "be normal" - denying that I had something going on that needed my attention. I didn't want it to be there, so I ignored it. I didn't want to be living in fear, that's not how I roll. I didn't expect it to stay, thought it would pass on when we got back into the swing of things... I was wrong.

Eventually I began identifying that I was experiencing complex anxiety. It was turning up in physical symptoms as well as mental and emotional symptoms. Finally, I reached out for some counselling which helped ease the edge of it off temporarily. I made it through the end of my degree year and Christmas, 2020. In a fog of dogged determination, I pulled myself together, turned a blind eye to the uncomfortable feelings, and started building my new career path that the training had been towards.

Despite still being wracked with self-doubt and fear, I managed to set up several projects which I was inspired about, and had a timeline of work stretching out in front of me for the next twelve months - that felt good. Then mid-2021, Delta hit. I got the flu, (which tested negative for COVID-19), but still wiped me out for a month or more. New Zealand's new, on-going lockdowns stopped my projects one after another. They were postponed, Postponed, POSTPoned, CANCELLED, like so many dominoes. I couldn't start anything new in the unknown circumstances. It became paralyzing.

Again, my thoughts oscillated between natural disappointment and a sense of gratitude that at least I didn't have it as bad as so many others. This was a global event after all, not my fault. Why did I feel so bad? This time, the waves didn't just suck the sand out from under my feet, it was more like a tsunami. All my support structures around me were in disarray as well. What I can now identify (wasn't so easy at the time) as major anxiety, gripped me hard. I was just feeling helpless, hopeless, semi-depressed, and immobilized. On the outside I tried to maintain a cheerful positivity. No point in being glum about that which we can't change. Rah rah rah.

Gripped with heart palpitations, irrational fear, and borderline agoraphobia - (which I had healed from as a young adult and not experienced in over twenty five years!), it felt like all the different anxieties and traumas I had ever known reared their ugly heads all at once, to be healed all over again. I was shocked. Quite frankly, I was in denial for many months. This couldn't possibly be happening to me - *I know better!*
Ha! *Yeah, right.*

Ah ha! Knowing is not doing. Knowing is not being. It was time for me to remember how to action what I know. What good is knowing techniques for stress management, if you don't actually live them? I'd been down this

"knowing but not applying" road before. Time to be
body, not just in my head.

When I noticed that PTSD Awareness Day was coming up,
I felt a strong urge to research and write an article for
Disruptive Author Magazine. What a healing journey that
ended up being! The anxiety and immobilization I had
been experiencing from the COVID-19 lockdowns were
actually signals of childhood traumas being re-triggered. I
had PTSD without even realizing. The many iterations of
writing that article became a source of healing guidelines
for me to follow myself. The golden rule came full circle, in
an effort to support others experiencing trauma, I
resourced myself to live my own healing practices again,
daily.

Going forward, I promise myself, I am remembering (and
learning fresh approaches too), to be LIVING the way of
self-care. For example, instead of rushing about trying to
keep up with outward deadlines and expectations, I am
stilling. I breathe deeply and allow myself space and time
to walk in Nature. If my body aches, or my head can't
think, I can drink more water, change my focus, be
conscious of my movement, or lack of movement, be
careful about what foods I keep in the pantry and fridge
so that my choices can't get too far off the "good for me"
track. Most importantly I have surrendered to the need to
sleep at different times than the tick-tock world expects. I
am allowing my own rhythms to show me the way I work
best.

It is early days. Sometimes it feels such unfamiliar territory to be trusting myself, trusting my body's wisdom. Feels uncomfortable to claim the space and time to be me being me. Even though, for years, I studied and taught that we must listen to what our bodies are trying to tell us, I am still a beginner. The Zen masters will tell us that Beginner's Mind is essential to any learning. Well here I am, in 'middle age', learning at last to be authentic to my own needs - even when inconvenient to myself or others. Learning to look after me: only then can I be of any use to anyone else anyway, so it's hardly selfish, (the selfish feeling still hangs around though - time to cut that string!) Learning to be comfortable and real, exploring, "What does that even look like and feel like anyway?"

So while the journey of COVID-19 and lockdowns has not been an easy walk in the park, it is a journey for which I am most grateful. From now on, I can live a healthier and more authentic life through the learning that has been triggered during this time, and the lessons put into practice.

Being Positive

by Sue

Sue is a retired teacher who has also written four self-help books and coaches women who want to make changes in their lives. She has been married to Greg for forty years and has a son and a daughter and four grandchildren.

We live in Brighton - where some of the earliest cases of COVID-19 were first identified (one of them being a doctor at our local surgery). We didn't think much about it. I suspected it would be bad news if I got it because I have bronchiectasis - a lung disorder which means I cough a lot and get quite poorly if I catch a cold.

Our son and family live in America and we flew to visit them on March 10th, 2020, despite some people warning us that the virus was becoming more widespread. We had only been in Austin for five days when one of their friends told us that Trump was issuing a ban on flights to the UK. We quickly changed our flights and flew home, still thinking that the dangers were exaggerated and that all our plans for the future were being thwarted because of something we thought would turn out to be a scare story. Our son, however, immediately closed his office and told his staff to work from home. He then sold his house and rented one with a swimming pool in rural Texas. He was concerned about his wife who has Type 1 diabetes and said he'd rather think he had done everything he could to keep his family safe, even if it turned out to be unnecessary.

Soon after our return, our grandchildren's school closed and our daughter and son-in-law had to work from home. We were used to providing childcare but now we were no longer allowed to do this and had to wave from their garden on our granddaughter's fourth birthday at the end of March 2020. We had short holidays booked in Berlin and Paris (the Berlin hotel immediately refunded our money but the Paris hotel refused). We had also booked a three-week holiday, in August, in Mykonos and Santorini with the whole family joining us for a week. The Mykonos hotel was cancelled and of course our son and family could not leave the States. We still went to Santorini with our daughter and family. Most of the time we were the only ones staying at the small family hotel. I don't remember worrying about COVID-19 at all as life seemed to be continuing as normal and the Greek residents were as relaxed and friendly as usual. Masks had to be worn in shops and restaurants but we ate outside and rarely had to wear them.

During lockdown we followed all the rules and were happy gardening and creating three vegetable beds, which turned out to be quite productive. I took the opportunity to de-clutter our house (where we have lived for over thirty years). I offered most things on our local Freecycle site - leaving them on the doorstep so that there was no contact. Lockdown gave me time to think and have the uninterrupted time to do this and to realise how much stuff we had that we did not need or use.

My closest friend, Chris, who had dementia, was very confused by the rules and continued to call round everyday and was bemused by having to chat on the doorstep. We went away again in October 2020 to Kefalonia, where we were immediately faced with a hurricane which flooded our hotel and smashed up our hire car. This was a freak occurrence as it is not known for this kind of weather. We extended our stay there to a month as everyone at home said the virus was rife and we felt very safe where we were. On our return we found Chris had been diagnosed with cancer and in November 2020 she died. There was torrential rain at her funeral, everyone wore masks, and there was no time, or place, to talk about her and her many achievements.

At the beginning of December 2020, new government guidelines allowed us to form a 'bubble' with our daughter and family for childcare. I met friends for walks and we got our first vaccinations. Schools opened, everyone wore masks and restaurants and pubs were given incentives by the government to encourage us to eat out. Like many other people at this time we felt we now had time to devote to a pet, so just before Christmas we adopted two adorable kittens from a rescue centre.

My ninety-one-year-old mother-in-law in Yorkshire became ill and my husband went by train to visit her in hospital. She died in February 2021 and we drove without stopping until we reached the Premier Inn in Barnsley which was the only place we could find that was open. We turned on the local news which declared that Barnsley was the COVID-19 hotspot of the UK. After the funeral, attended only by the two of us and Greg's brother and family, we drove straight back to Brighton, again with no opportunity to talk or mix with the others.

We had our second and third vaccinations and, although more and more people we knew seemed to be getting COVID-19, none of them seemed to suffer with much more than a bad cold. In June 2021 we had another long holiday in Corfu. Again there were very few British people on the island and life is lived outdoors. We heard that the Greek government had decided that residents of the islands should all be full vaccinated and since everyone had to show proof of vaccination before getting on a plane to Greece and have random temperature checks, we felt safer than we did at home.

In August 2021, we took our grandson on holiday to Boscombe and went to the cinema for the first time and ate in restaurants, probably our riskiest time of the pandemic. Before the pandemic we used to go to our health club three times a week (I do aquarobics and my husband runs) but it closed for about ten months. This probably impacted on my level of fitness but I can't say that it affected my mental health, as I continued to feel personally, albeit guiltily, content throughout the pandemic.

Our son and family had finally been able to visit us, after moving first to Portland and then to Florida in June 2021. They had big decisions to make about where they wanted to live as he realised he could run his business quite happily from anywhere in the world. Their children had not been to school since they first left Austin but seemed to have thrived with home schooling. We had kept in touch with weekly Zoom calls. They were delighted with our two kittens but the cats were not as keen on our daughter-in-law's assistance dog (which had accompanied them on the plane from America).

We were able to attend a twice-postponed family wedding in Yorkshire in August 2021. We had been asked to wear masks for the ceremony but half of the guests did not bother. (We did). We then drove to Tenby, in Wales, to stay with a friend. On the way we stayed overnight in hotels in Buxton and Crickhowell. We felt as though life was at last returning to normal and that the virus was beginning to go away.

We booked a holiday in Crete in October 2021 with the whole family joining us for a week for my seventieth birthday. Again it felt a much safer place to be than the UK and a lot quieter than Brighton and holiday spots at home. Our son and family stayed with us for four months before moving back to the States in November 2021 to live in Serenbe, Georgia. We visited them in March 2022, exactly two years since we had to cut short our visit to Austin because of COVID-19.

They had both caught COVID-19 before our visit but were not too ill. Our daughter-in-law was given a drug, Paxlovid, which seemed effective. Meanwhile our daughter, in Brighton, also tested positive and is still suffering from Long Covid and signed off work. Her doctor is sympathetic but there seems to be little evidence of anything alleviating the symptoms of bouts of complete exhaustion, muscle fatigue and 'brain fog'. She enjoys her job as a researcher for a domestic abuse charity and worries about losing it if she doesn't get better quickly. We personally felt as though we had been very lucky and I think, perhaps, being able to take holidays on Greek islands with very few tourists was one of the reasons.

On Monday 4th July 2022, I started with my usual bronchial cough and an unbelievable tiredness that meant I slept most of the day. I quickly saw the doctor and explained we were going on holiday the next day and I didn't want to be ill. She gave me antibiotics for two weeks and told me to stay out of the sun. We arrived in Majorca in the early hours of Wednesday morning and discovered that our friends from Scotland were staying in the same town. My husband decided to take a COVID-19 test as he was feeling lethargic and off his food. I couldn't believe it when he tested positive. I took one too and it was also positive. As a result we were unable to meet our friends as we tested positive every day for a week.

The main thing I have learned from this whole experience is how important it is to be self-sufficient. I don't mean in terms of food, I mean that you have to be happy in your own company and with the person/people you live with. We have always been close to our children and grandchildren and the enforced separation, particularly from our American family, was very difficult despite being able to keep in contact via Zoom. I know that I have been extremely lucky during the pandemic and I feel quite guilty. I am very sorry for all the people who have suffered so much during this time. Let's hope it soon becomes a distant memory.

Flight to France

by Jill Stevens

Jill Stevens used to be a journalist. Later she was Director of Consumer Affairs for an international company. She worked with debt advice charities and the government as a consumer education specialist explaining how the financial sector worked and how to avoid becoming the victim of identity fraud. She is married to Roger.

Deserted. First the M23, then the M26, then the M20 and finally the Eurotunnel terminal at Folkestone. We felt as if we were driving through a post-apocalyptic film set. It was scary – but strangely exciting.

As we drove through the barrier, our van was electronically recognised and our arrival was registered remotely. At the first checkpoint the British guy, masked and gloved – as, indeed, we were – waved us through. "Good luck."

We drove up to the French immigration booth. I handed over our passports and the papers we had downloaded from the French government website, signing to our essential reason for travel. Having a house in France was not enough. We hoped the fact that we were desperate to be with my ninety-three year old mother would be. And that a separate paper I had written in French explaining her frailty would be convincing.

It was. After much chin rubbing, the official eventually waved us through and we and one other car were allowed on the train. The six other cars we saw were not so lucky. They were refused entry to France, turned around and headed back to Folkestone.

This was 20th March 2020. France had been in lockdown for three days. British people had been told by our Prime Minister on the 16th, "Now is the time for everyone to stop non-essential contact and travel." But on that day

France had closed. "We are once again at war," President Emmanuel Macron announced, "not fighting against any army, nor against any other nation. But the enemy is there, invisible, elusive, advancing."

Indeed it was. We had a ferry crossing booked. That was cancelled. Panic abounded but Eurotunnel was still operating. And we made it. I thought we would be with my mother for a few months, seeing her through lockdown. After all, our Prime Minister had said the day before our dash to the Tunnel, "Britain can turn the tide of COVID-19 in 12 weeks."

Nearly thirty months later, we're still in France. We had to become French residents in order to stay with my mother, as Brexit hit during the pandemic. I suppose the copious amounts of paperwork that I dealt with, in order to make myself, my husband, my mother and my brother (and our pets) legal immigrants, was one way to combat the boredom of isolation.

Lucky enough to be in an old farmhouse – crumbling but more or less watertight and with a large garden out in the countryside, meant we could enjoy the lovely weather in 2020. We had plums galore. And tomatoes the size of melons. And loads of figs. We grew beans. We made jam and chutney and pickles. This isolation lark was quite fun. My husband will elucidate, in his chapter, on how we entertained ourselves and our friends thanks to the Internet and social media.

But not all was good in the garden. Confinement, as it was called in France, was fiercely enforced and strictures were many. We could walk the dog – but no more than one kilometre from our house. We could order our groceries online and drive to pick them up in the local town: park by a machine in a bay, swipe our card, open the boot and wait for an assistant, in mask/visor and gloves to load our order, close our own boot and drive off. We were advised to wash all packaging, which we did. What a chore. The only shops open were food stores and pharmacies. Even several boulangeries closed their doors – supplies were disrupted and no self-respecting French baker would profer a sub-standard baguette.

Each time we left the house we had to fill in and sign an "attestation" citing which of about five essential reasons meant we should be allowed to stray. Food, medicine and checking on dependent relatives were the main ones. The form included name, address, date and place of birth – and we were allowed to stay out for an hour. We were curfewed after 6pm. We were not able to stay in the same house as my mother and brother, but we visited daily, parking our van close to their kitchen and talking through the open window.

I guess it was all a bit of an adventure for the first few months and we were okay. We all sat tight and waited to hear how the scientists' rapid search for a vaccine was getting on.

What was not fun at all was the effect lockdown had on my mother. Her memory was already failing. The fear of the virus and her confusion around the rules, accelerated her dementia. We tried to keep things from her, but she caught snippets on the television and from our conversations. Sadly, she didn't really understand and would often wake in the night, petrified that the gendarmes were coming to arrest her. Or that we would be put in prison if we were caught going to collect her medicine from the pharmacy. Or that everyone in the world was going to die. Her anxiety was continual and excruciating for her and for us.

By 2021 we had enjoyed a short spell of freedom – the one kilometre we were allowed to travel had been stretched to twenty kilometres and then to two hundred and fifty. We ventured out in our camper van for a few days in the Vendée, to the east of us. With food in the van's fridge, we could remain isolated and safely walk the dog in deserted countryside.

While our travelling distance had been limited to twenty kilometres, I had taken a pair of compasses and drawn a circle around our house. We had explored most of the allowed area! At that time my mum was well enough to enjoy a trip out. But gradually her condition deteriorated. Dementia is a cruel disease.

The weeks and the months wore on. The novelty wore off. I was desperate to see my son and daughter-in-law, and my grandson, whom I had watched on Zoom and FaceTime change from a young ten-year-old to a leggy adolescent. When we left England, he was shorter than me and had a lovely treble singing voice. Now he is taller than his grandfather and sounds like a man. I've missed more than two years of his transition from child to teenager. Yes, I resent that.

While we've been forced to stay away, my brother has had treatment for cancer, several friends have died – both from COVID-19 and other causes. I've not been there to comfort anyone, or to be comforted, or to help single friends who found isolation very hard. We've made huge use of Zoom and FaceTime – but people need a hug. I'm no different in this respect to most – we've all been denied access to our friends and family and for many it has been much, much harder than it has been for me. But being abroad meant we couldn't even mask up and wave from the other side of the road or go for a distanced walk together once that was allowed.

The decisions made by Boris Johnson and his colleagues have, to me, beggared belief. My opinion of him and his government has been worsened by Brexit – a move that I consider suicidal for the UK economy, truly damaging to the opportunities for young people, detrimental to almost all aspects of British society and a blow to peace in Europe. It has forced half of my family to have to be domiciled in a foreign country. It's a disaster and it came at an already very stressful time.

I am clinically extremely vulnerable, so a visit to England now – we live in a big city – poses quite a risk. Despite my three vaccinations and a booster, my doctor has told me not to attend indoor events; I continue to wear a mask and to distance where I can; I am nervous, visiting England, as a I watch people return to 'normal' life, hustling and bustling along the streets, sneezing on buses, hugging and huddling. COVID-19 may be over for most people. And I understand that we have to learn to live with the virus and that herd immunity might work for many. But for me the risk of being very ill if I catch COVID-19 remains and my fear is real.

We are in England as I write. We'll soon be back in France, where restrictions are gradually lifting, although some people continue to wear masks in the markets and they are still required in many shops. Restaurants and cafés have been open for some time, albeit with tables moved further apart.

All this is too late for my mum, who died in January 2022. It is sad that her last years were marred by the pandemic and all that it brought. But thank goodness we were allowed to spend those years with her – thanks to the common sense of a French immigration official who told us more than two years ago: "Allez, allez. Vous pouvez entrer."

The Show Must Go On
by Roger Stevens

Roger Stevens is an award-winning children's poet and author with more than forty books to his name. He is also a musician and songwriter and has released several albums. He lives in Brighton and France with his wife, Jill and their very shy dog Jasper.

In normal times, I visit schools to give poetry performances and run workshops for children and teachers. As the virus hit, schools closed, most children stayed at home and education became something you accessed online.

But I carried on. I used my phone to record poetry readings, workshops and advice on creative writing. I posted videos to YouTube. These were used by teachers and parents grappling with home schooling. Modern technology meant I could do all this from France, where my wife and I were locked down.

And although we, like so many people, missed our family and freedoms, I feel duty bound to admit that there was a lot about being isolated that I enjoyed. I was very lucky to have somewhere to flee to with a garden. COVID-19 had no real financial impact on us, being retired. I had my piano and guitar to play with. And the Internet...

While working with teachers, it occurred to me that one thing closed schools could not deliver was morning assembly. Now, some of you might think that's a good thing. Certainly, the assemblies I experienced as a child fail to feature as my favourite school memories. Although the pigeon flying in through a window was pretty good.

Being a determinedly cheerful person and someone who loves comedy, I realised we could have fun with this. I enlisted the help of my wife, Jill. She didn't need too much persuading to play several parts in the series of five videos we made for YouTube. She was variously Ms Featherstonehaugh (pronounced Fanshaw), Deputy Head of St Groat's Academy, and a visiting vicar. I was Mr Cholmondeley (pronounced Chumley), Headteacher and a visiting poet.

Why we have a supply of wigs and odd clothes chez nous I'm not sure. But we do. Those and Jill's make up helped us make five videos, one for each day of the week. Feedback suggested we made a lot of people happy. Although I suspect they didn't fall over laughing like we did while recording.

During the week we learn more about Mr Sprog, who gets lost on the school trip to France. We are told that it wasn't Mr Green seen going into the cinema with Ms Scarlett but "somebody who looked a bit like him". There's a petition to change class names. And music for the assemblies is chosen by pupils. As the week progresses, the assemblies become more chaotic and we begin to suspect what the deputy head feels passionate about.

The YouTube link for series of ten-minute videos is below. https://www.youtube.com/results?search_query=st+groats+academy

I also made a lot of music while in France. I missed playing live as a singer-songwriter, as most musicians did, but I continued to help organise and play at our monthly Roots Folk Club – a complicated collection of videos from performers across the country and a Zoom audience with members from around the world. As we're usually Sussex based, this was quite an expansion and meant we could reconnect with old members of the folk club who had moved to Wales and Scotland! And I did manage to make an album using my favourite recording studio long distance.

I wrote eleven songs for *Rescued by Orcas* and recorded them, singing and playing guitar. What an amazing invention is the Smartphone! I sent the songs, via the Internet, to record producer Ali Gavan. Also a musician, he added bass guitar and drums. My friend, the esteemed Charlotte Glasson visited the studio in between lockdowns and added saxophone and flute. Andy Melrose emailed some mandolin to Ali and together we mixed the album online.

The physical CD was made in Brighton. I advertised it via social media. In the absence of a working distribution department, another friend, who was staying in our Hove flat, posted the CDs to customers. Isn't it amazing what you can do these days without actually being there!?

I tried to keep the songs "uppy." But some of the gloom that was around during the pandemic inevitably crept in. The lyrics to one of the songs, *Splendid Isolation,* can be found below.

I think the pandemic did give us some thinking time. It did slow life down a bit. And for many, like us, whose lifestyle could be described as hectic, that was a good thing. As a writer I am a solitary worker. As a composer, too, I usually work alone. So while I missed the camaraderie of playing on stage, I found the enforced stay-at-home time with not much to do but write and play music, rather welcome.

For people not so used to self-contemplation, for the do-ers, people who like to be out and about in the community, campaigning and working with others – people like my wife – isolation was undoubtedly much more difficult to cope with. Jill moved her work for good causes online, but I know she missed the companionship of like-minded friends. For people in sub-standard housing, stuck indoors with young children, with too little money, who lost their jobs or were furloughed – it was horrendous. So I count myself very, very fortunate.

Communities came together during the first lockdown. Did we really believe, 'we're all in this together'? Some people recalled the camaraderie of the war, although I always felt that was pushing it. In the UK everyone clapped the NHS. How well they were doing, how brave they were.

We were encouraged to cheer our heroes by a government which was making life as difficult as possible for the health service as they could, giving bogus contracts and millions of pounds to their cronies who couldn't deliver the equipment that our doctors and nurses so desperately needed. Boris Johnson and his Cabinet who, in my opinion at the time – since borne out by the courts – dealt with the whole thing very badly if not criminally.

So things were beginning to pall by the second year – for us and for everyone. Our road's WhatsApp group continues to share messages, but it's different. Still in France, we made very few videos in year two. I did a few things for schools, but the mood was definitely darker. The weather wasn't as good. Our crops failed. We missed our family more. And the pandemic seemed like it would never end.

Splendid Isolation

We do our best, but we're all alone
Just a thinking machine, some skin and bone
We make a few friends, help the human race carry on.

Well I hope it ain't a shock
But for your information
Every single one of us is in... Splendid Isolation

Is life an illusion, is life a test?
I've been looking for the answers and I've asked the very best
Guru on the mountain top, the girl in the chippy
The singer who spent a day too long in Mississippi

Well I hope it ain't a shock
But for your information
Every single one of us is in... Splendid Isolation

I hold you in my arms
And we're living in the moment
As the world drifts by
You'll find us here, with an ice-cold beer
Looking for that comet
Low in the Northern sky

You come into the world with nothing, you take nothing
when you go
Like to think there's a life hereafter
Wouldn't we all like to know
Buddha said it, Jesus said it, Mohammed said it too
Got to love your neighbour, that's all you got to do

Well I hope it ain't a shock
But for your information
Every single one of us is in... Splendid Isolation

It's time the human race passed its graduation
Extend the hand of friendship – nation unto nation
Listen to the news – you get filled with consternation
Bombs and guns and fear and hate, the final conflagration
It's not odd that you think you're all alone, you're
searching for salvation
Every single one of us is in
Splendid Isolation

The album is called Rescued by Orcas. You can listen to it on https://rogerstevens.bandcamp.com/album/rescued-by-orcas or buy it at www.rogerstevensshop.com

I want my old life back
by Christine

Christine is a semi- retired tutor living in Stourbridge in the West Midlands. She said that her husband's sudden retirement and a new puppy sounded reasonably pleasant and would be positive life changes. But these, together with a visceral fear of COVID-19 left her completely overwhelmed, threatening her marriage and mental stability.

The start of it all

It was only a sore throat to begin with, the kind you get before 'flu. It was just before March 2020, so it seemed out of season and unexpected. We put it down to work pressures and had recently agreed that a three-day week was more suitable for my fifty-eight-year-old husband, Ian. We were in the early weeks of this change, and he was worried that the company would just allocate five days' work into three. He had been extremely busy in previous months, as the persistent flooding had required him to travel hundreds of miles in his loss-adjusting appointments. On Thursday March 5th he was feeling particularly unwell. He had recently met up with claimants in Shrewsbury on a chilly morning and was forced to hang around an indoor market, where people were already fist-bumping each other in view of incoming news of a highly transmissible new virus. He was tired and headachy, as well as sore-throated, but my lovely husband (and caring stepdad to my two children) was still willing to travel all the way to Cardiff from the West Midlands, to answer a distress call we had from my daughter. For the same reason, I had to cancel a tutorial I was giving that day (I work as a private English tutor), so the date is a memorable one. It marked the date of a new beginning. Life was about to change, not least because it was the day we picked up Bertie and brought him home.

A New Puppy

A few weeks earlier, and in a bid to cheer ourselves up, we took ourselves out in the car to Stourport to look at a puppy with a view to buying him. This idea was after years of deliberation. Ian had always wanted a dog, while I was less certain. In the early years of our relationship, both in our second marriages, we had enjoyed many holidays and travels abroad and I loved the freedom from responsibility this created. It seemed that the nicest hotels and B&Bs would not allow pets and air travel would be impossible. I was loath to give all this up for the responsibility of a dog. However, in more recent years we tended to stay home for vacations (even before "staycations" became a must) and were enjoying visiting Dorset, Cornwall and places in Wales and Scotland. With both of us now working part-time and from home, it seemed the right time to reconsider.

It was a beautiful litter of Cockapoo puppies, all very similar, but Bertie immediately settled on my lap and the rest is history. I was smitten. He chose me, or so I like to believe. When we returned a few weeks later, social distancing was already in place and he was again placed in my lap, this time while I was still in the car. He would not look me in the eye at first but cuddled up nonetheless and went to sleep.

The Cough

Ian had a few more rough days after his trip to Shrewsbury, with a slight fever, fatigue and later a cough which persisted well beyond the other symptoms and into the third week. Surprisingly, he managed to work through those early days, despite feeling unwell, for fear of the backlog which would develop otherwise. Around this time there was news of a new virus, otherwise known as COVID-19, which had developed in Wuhan, China in January, with the first known cases in the UK arriving on the 28th of February 2020.

It's Official

On the 11th of March 2020, the COVID-19 outbreak was officially declared to have arrived in the UK. It was my birthday on the 18th and social distancing was already in place, with advice not to hug people outside your household "bubble". I did hug my children, who both live away, but cancelled the planned dinner out with the rest of the family. Instead, the four of us had a take-away meal at our house. By the 20th March, pubs, restaurants and sports halls were closed, along with schools and colleges. I cancelled all my tutorials, which were face-to-face. By the 23rd March we were in a "loose" lockdown, under the new Coronavirus Act 2020.

Boris

In late March we heard that our Prime Minister, Boris Johnson had developed symptoms. He was admitted to hospital on April 5th and put in ICU the next day. It seemed very serious for a while, but he was back on the wards on the 9th and sent home to Chequers on the 12th, looking quite frail.

Struggles at Home

It was April 1st and Ian was working from home in his office, leaving me in full charge of our two-month-old puppy. It was very tiring, watching him like a hawk, as he couldn't jump down from the sofa he liked to lie on. He needed to wee after waking up, after eating, or when excited, amounting to a tiny teaspoonful on the carpet each time. I spent all day mopping up, playing with him and cuddling him. It was a full-time job and I was exhausted, reflecting that I was probably too old for this at sixty-six. This continued for two more days until Ian finished work and I couldn't wait to share the load! He did take over almost immediately but the challenge of attending to Bertie was beginning to test our relationship.

By April 4th, we had established a certain routine whereby Bertie relied on me as a bed, feeder and entertainer. He followed me round the house continuously: a 'Velcro' puppy. It was lovely but exhausting. We had nappy pads on the floors of our kitchen and living room. At this point I felt sufficiently equipped to cope and had no idea that this was nothing compared to the 'toddler' stage that was about to begin!

Another week and Bertie was getting bigger, more independent and more boisterous. He could go up the steps from the garden to the patio but not get down again by himself – a bit like the sofa. We could see that he was strong willed and still did not answer to his name. He would "sit"and understood "no" although this is not a word recommended by the experts!

In the following weeks we made several visits to the vet, as Bertie tried to play with a bee and got stung on his tongue and soon after developed an eye infection. Never a dull moment!

In the middle of all this, Ian resigned from work completely, planning a happy retirement after thirty-five years as a Loss Adjuster. Although we had discussed this at length and I tried to be supportive, I was not initially happy with this. There were big financial concerns, in fact we might have to move - we found ourselves together in the house 24/7, like never before!

My Illness

On May 9th it was my son's birthday. This was a subdued affair – he came to our garden and socially distanced, after he gave me a hug. Around the same time, I had a misunderstanding with my daughter, causing great upset to both of us for a couple of days. I was very upset and stressed over this, felt unwell, lightheaded and extremely fatigued until we sorted it out.

On May 11th Ian bought a new car (actually an old one), having said goodbye to the company Mondeo (a new one). On May 14th we went on a trip to Bewdley in the new car, hoping to have a nice walk around with Bertie. But when we arrived at the car park, we found it was jam-packed with people, making it impossible to socially distance. I felt terrified and after about ten minutes I just wanted to go home, abandoning any idea of a leisurely afternoon by the river. It was an extremely hot day, so on returning home we decided to sit in the garden in the sunshine. However, I soon began to feel very unwell: very hot, with a severe headache, so decided to go and lie down inside. I then discovered I had an exceedingly high temperature.

The next day I still had a temperature, headache and fatigue and couldn't lift my head off the pillow, not even to cuddle Bertie. On the third day I still felt unwell – is it COVID-19? I rang 111 and soon got referred to a doctor who told me it might be COVID-19. My temperature was high and my pulse was racing at 120 bpm. I ordered a test and decided to isolate, so Ian slept in the spare room. On the fourth day I felt slightly better, my headache had gone but I had a weird tenderness at the top of my back when I moved around.

The next day (18th May) there was still tenderness in my back, but I was generally improving. The test arrived, which was easier to perform than expected, but I still felt still fatigued, with no energy left to play with Bertie. Finally I began to feel a bit more like myself with my temperature near normal. My test came back negative. I was relieved and tearful. What was it then – sunstroke or stress?

Living under Restrictions

There were various news items relating to COVID-19 over the following weeks. Some people were flouting lockdown, politicians were blaming other politicians over COVID-19 prevention measures. Around the world, lockdowns were established much sooner than ours and there were routine checks for COVID-19 at airport checkpoints. Different strategies applied for Wales, Scotland and Ireland in comparison with England.

Ian was disappointed about the loss of restaurants and my daughter about the closing of gyms, whilst I was just glad there was no option, because I was becoming increasingly reclusive. Hubby went out regularly to do the shopping and I constantly reminded him to wash his hands when he came in! I didn't want any social gatherings and only went out to walk the dog for a quiet fifteen minutes at a time in our local park. Even then I was reluctant to speak to other dog walkers, relying on the lead length for social distancing, although I was aware that Bertie needed to

PART I
PANDEMIC STORIES

mix with other dogs and was keen to do so! I was becoming more confident about this before my illness. Since then, although my test was negative, I have been just as anxious, if not more so. I did not want to get ill again, and it was not a mild attack, whatever it was. They call this "Coronaphobia" and I am probably a classic example.

The Easing of Rules

June 1st 2020 was a date set to begin the re-opening of schools, under social distancing and mask-wearing rules, and with only Years One and Six attending to begin with. Later, all schools reopened but with the usual restrictions. Shortly after this I recommended tutoring, but only online. Visits from one member of another household were allowed, provided it was outdoors. At first, this had to be in a public place, but later on, gardens become an acceptable alternative. It was wonderful to be able to have our children over to visit. Non-essential shops were allowed to open mid-June, but businesses requiring more extreme social distancing such as hairdressers, pubs, restaurants, gyms and dentists had to wait until early July. By then the roads seem to be as busy as ever, giving a feeling that a lot of people were returning to their normal lives.

However, I was still very cautious, rarely visiting a shop or restaurant, relying on grocery deliveries and the odd take-away for food and my ever-loving and supportive husband for any day-to-day purchases. It now seemed fortuitous that he resigned when he did – how would I have coped? Thank goodness also for Bertie. He had become very attached to both of us, wanting to please us (most of the time) and did what we told him (most of the time). I cannot imagine life without him now, even though he drives me crazy sometimes with his loud bark and his energetic and occasionally destructive ways!

It is now February 2022, and I have not recorded anything since July 2020. All restrictions have been removed and the country has opened up again. I am slowly and cautiously getting out and about, grateful to have survived in one piece, and happy with my boys (Hubby and Bertie).

But it's been a bumpy ride!

Melbourne, the world's most liveable city

by Ross

Ross (not his real name) is a UK born (now Australian) teacher who left Norfolk in 2017 for a new adventure. Little did he know that this adventure would entail lockdowns, mandatory quarantine and becoming a master of teaching "over the air." Not quite the adventure he had in mind!

"Melbourne – The world's most liveable city and the most locked down."

Moving to Melbourne in January 2018 after working in the UK, I was told this was the best city to live in – bars, culture, nightlife and the arts were all represented here. Whilst it took a while to get used to the grimy city centre, having moved from Norfolk via Perth in Western Australia, I gradually grew to realise that some truth existed in these proclamations. I could see, in many ways, why this city had held the coveted title of the world's most liveable city for three years in succession.

Fast forward to January 2020 and, in preparation for our belated wedding reception in Norfolk and with flights booked, we did not really take much notice of this new virus which was sweeping China. However, by the beginning of March things were changing rapidly and, with only one week before our departure, our Australian PM decided to close the International Borders. Australians and Permanent Residents Overseas had less than one week to make their way home. We were now banned from leaving Australia and could only do so with prior governmental approval. Only a few weeks after this, mandatory hotel quarantine was introduced and then the dreaded caps on incoming passengers. A lucky escape for my husband and I, as some thirty thousand Australians would become stranded overseas, some for more than six months.

In less than three months, the city, once vibrant and a haven of eclectic cafes, restaurants and bars, became a ghost town. The Central Business District (CBD) was permanently closed and would, in fact, be in a state of closure and partial closure for the next year. Yet, at the beginning no one could have guessed the severity of what was to come.

Apart from the inconvenience of not getting one's hair cut on the famous Collins Street, there was little to impact upon those of us who were considered "regional." A mere forty-five kilometres from the CBD was like a different world. However, as with all things during 2020 and 2021, there was a constant flux in rules and regulations, with most people respecting the decisions of our "betters".

As teachers, we were instructed to "educate online" and, having been given some hastily arranged ICT professional development on Zoom, we were, for want of a better word, sent forth to continue our trade. In all honesty, the first weeks went well as students and teachers relished the ability to teach and learn from home. Those who had previously travelled up to forty minutes to reach school were happy to be able to roll out of bed, shower and be at the computer in less than thirty minutes. Nevertheless, cracks were soon making their appearance. Student interest waned, teachers were less able to engage their classes and the realisation came upon us that learning and teaching was a craft which could only be practised in the traditional way, face to face.

Even more tangible evidence of this new situation was the fact that regional and metro, were now going to be divided, like Berlin during the Cold War era. The Premier of the State directed that on all roads into and out of the city of Melbourne, police roadblocks were to be established and all cars stopped. The infamous "Ring of Steel" was born. During this time, movement between regional and metro was curtailed to 'essential' travel only. All schools, hospitals and businesses which were allowed to operate during this time, were required to issue state approved 'passes' which, in effect, served to prove that the holder was entitled to cross the demarcation line to perform their approved business. This was something which freedom loving Australians found hard to stomach and, from a personal point of view, one of the main contributing factors to the rise in the level of discontent which was steadily increasing by the day.

This lasted for a good three months before, with the approach of Christmas and the end of the 2020 school year, senior classes were once again allowed into schools. Each day, the Premier of Victoria would announce the grim figures of death and hospitalisations. However, the figures soon became less and less significant – unless, of course, one was personally touched by an individual who made up this statistic. By virtue of the sheer numbers, we had become desensitised to the "new norm". Most people's thoughts were turning towards the arrival of summer and the knowledge that with it would come a decline in the hospitalisations and deaths. Summer would herald a reduction in case numbers as it had done in the Northern Hemisphere a few months previously.

Unlike the UK, public examinations in Australia went ahead in all states and territories. End of year celebrations were less joyous and elaborate compared to previous years. No longer were schools booking out whole restaurants and our traditional event at the Marvel Stadium in the city was replaced by onsite activities. Christmas 2020 was merely the end of a year which most Melbournians wanted to forget. By that time, the state and city had been locked down twice for a total of one hundred and sixty four dark days. We welcomed 2021 with the hope of better things to come and there was a genuine hope that we had lived through the worst.

No sooner had 2021 began than it was clear that this hope had been misplaced. The return to school increased cases dramatically and within weeks the new "short and sharp" approach closed workplaces again. Indeed, it was the return to schools across the state which would send us into our third state-wide lockdown. This would be the phenomenon to which we would become accustomed in the coming months.

Personally, with no need to enter the Central Business District (CBD), I was only a bystander. However, in July 2021 I had no option but to brave the city and the risk it entailed, to complete my Australian Citizenship interview and test at one of the only government offices still operating. This was during one of the short windows of opportunity when businesses were once again open and those who dared could move freely between the city and outlying areas. With airport style security and the double-checking of vaccine certificates on our phones, the day passed uneventfully. Most people scuttled to and fro, interaction between them was minimal, and masks were mandated in all areas. On this one day, it was so evident that the city, once vibrant and constantly on the move, was suffering more than I had ever thought possible. The iconic trams of the city, which once rattled though the streets taking office workers and tourists to their destinations, reminded me of the death rattle which one hears in the hours before the arrival of death. Was this an audible clue that this once great city was entering its final moments? Hopefully not, however this was 2021 and nothing could be predicted with any certainty.

The next day, despite all our collective efforts to be safe, the inevitable occurred. All colleagues at my workplace were sent home with the instruction to isolate. One of our colleagues had tested positive and had been at work, which resulted in each person on site being forced into mandatory fourteen-day home isolation. However, it was not just teachers who were in compulsory isolations. Every student and their immediate family were now in the same position. With over two thousand five hundred students and their immediate families locked down at home, this was the first taste of what metro inhabitants had previously experienced.

Police and health team home visits followed to all, and in scenes reminiscent of World War Two, state funded relief parcels started to arrive at our door. Lessons continued online with the occasional day of respite. Lessons were punctuated with constant interruptions, as both students and teachers were called away to present themselves to the quarantine teams who did spot checks to ensure our compliance.

I had never needed to have recourse to charity in my life but when you have been sent home and unable to grab any supermarket delivery slots, then the concept of pride must be swallowed. Many welcomed food parcels, not because they were financially unable to buy food, but due to the rush on delivery slots. In addition, with many parents occupying service jobs and being quarantined, the supermarkets had a lack of staff to fulfil delivery.

It was at this point that us "regionals" really knew what the inner-city inhabitants had experienced in the previous lockdowns. Being legally mandated to remain at home with no personal liberty at all is an alien concept to most and certainly one which does not fit well with the Australian idea of freedom. As we watched, the mood of resentment and growing unhappiness started to manifest itself and continued to do so over the next few months. Rallies and demonstrations, hitherto unknown in the city, shut down many streets and areas. The city, once vibrant was becoming a place where one did not venture unless necessary, and only then for the least amount of time possible. Melbourne was going to be a place which would take years to recover its former glory – some even doubted that this was possible.

From a very personal perspective the past year, at that point, had really flown past with little of significance to make any time stand out. Birthday, gatherings, and simple jaunts away from home were never celebrated or undertaken; there was an ever-present fear, almost tangible, and certainly felt when one boarded a train or went outside to the supermarket. People did not mingle, talk and the rush to get things done and get to the safety of one's own home was certainly evident. Our local businesses were on their knees, as people became recluses and hermits at home. The mental health of many had suffered and this was evident both within schools and the general population.

With the arrival of vaccinations into Australia, a veritable and palpable sense of relief could be felt. Whilst the government in Canberra had been slow off the mark to order and distribute vaccination doses, in contrast to action of the UK government, when push came to shove, most Victorians were lining up to be vaccinated. Perhaps the dark days of lockdown was the main push factor here, although one could also argue that the impending mandates to be vaccinated for education and health care professionals were at the forefront of people's mind. The fear of being isolated even further as a result of choosing not to be vaccinated was the main factor for those who had a choice.

Perhaps it was, quite simply, the fact that on October 4th, 2021, Melbourne overtook Buenos Aires to claim the title of being the world's most locked down city. We will never know.

Looking back on these events, it is hard to believe how most people survived and tolerated what was the most draconian laws Australia has seen in recent years. For many who have experience of war and conflict, and there are many overseas born Australians who have, this was simply yet another arduous task to be endured without question or rebellion. However, rebellion and opposition certainly became part of the fabric of society towards the end of 2021. Anti-vaccine mandate demonstrations were to see violent clashes between public and police, something which Australia has rarely seen in her modern democratic society.

Australians have certainly become more prepared to question their political leaders and to hold them to account for their actions. The recent election of the Labour Party after eleven years in opposition, has shown that Australians, whilst cognisant of the need for the actions taken, do not always believe that these measures were proportionate to the threat. The Liberal government was, in effect, punished by the electorate who on May 21st 2022 were seeking a fresh start and a new approach.

COVID-19 has certainly not retreated and will be with us for many years to come. International visitors are slowly trickling back to the city and many Australians have taken the chance to take long postponed overseas trips. The cost to both the economy and individuals will be with us for decades, all political parties admit this. Nevertheless, a change is evident and new hope is rising from the despair created by 2020 and 2021.

Australians are known to be battlers and prepared to tough things out, as they would have to be, living on a land where fire and flood threaten every year. When I look around and see how resilient people are, I know that Melbourne will return to her former glory, but bearing the cicatrices of the pandemic. It may take a while, but like a phoenix rising from the ashes, so will Melbourne.

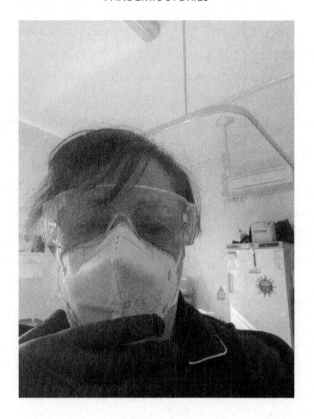

COVID-19 changed life as we know it
by Maria

Maria is a mother to two grown-up sons and grandmother to three young children. In amongst everything that has happened as a result of COVID-19, her younger son had his wedding cancelled twice because of lockdowns. Maria has worked in the NHS for over forty years.

If I'm honest, I really didn't pay much attention when stories started coming in about COVID-19. After all, it was prevalent in a country that the news had reported as having unconventional live animal markets, in unsanitary conditions. I thought it was a bit of hype ...how wrong I was!

It soon kicked off across countries all over the world in a most alarming way. The usually bustling cities were deserted, armed police were marshalling the streets, people were dying in unfathomable numbers, life as we knew it changed beyond all recognition. The impact was to be monumental. I was afraid, very afraid. Fearful for my family, friends and myself but also for mankind and for what would be left of the world after this 'thing' desecrated it. The isolation from people I loved was unbearable. The National Health Service was overwhelmed. MY NHS. The institution that my sister and I worked in tirelessly, as nurses.

I had a massive personal dilemma when I received notification from the government to say I should shield, due to several risk factors including asthma and sickle cell trait. I was so torn between my vocation and staying alive. I cried all day, as I just had no idea how to proceed. My decision would not only affect me, but also my children and young grandchildren. I couldn't bear not being there if I didn't make it through this COVID-19 crisis. Eventually a compromise was found, as I adapted to trying to "work from home", a new phrase that would soon become so familiar. However nursing and working from home is not a good combination. Nursing by phone and computer isn't my style. For one thing, many patients I spoke to were desperate, misinformed, petrified, lonely, stressed and depressed. I was possibly the only person that many had had contact with and I was torn between sticking to workloads I had been set and trying to comfort the faceless person at the end of a phone. Also, I was well aware that my sister was still working 'at the coal face' in an acute nursing setting which was putting her at risk, that she was experiencing marked allergic reactions to her PPE and having to take all kinds of treatments daily to allow her to continue to work. So proud of her for that!

After a few weeks and following discussions with my employers, I felt I had no choice but to return to the work-place. Working from home really didn't work for me or for the practice as, in the main, my work is very hands-on and we didn't want to delay preventative screening tests and treatment room care that is integral to my role. I know many doctors' surgeries didn't see patients in person, but we did carry on trying to proceed with as full a service as we could. Innovative new methods were brought into play, including e-consults, video-consults and so on.

Eventually, I got enough confidence to enrol so I could administer COVID-19 vaccinations, when I wasn't working at my regular job. I was so angry with the disruption to life that COVID-19 was causing, I decided life might return to normal more quickly if we got as many people vaccinated as possible. My sister also joined the fight and we went out to nursing homes and the housebound to vaccinate. We even vaccinated our mother, who was in a nursing home at the time. The vaccination team built an inspiringly positive ethos and we bonded as we united to fight this unwanted villain.

In the midst of trying to cope with the turmoil of emotions and missing precious time with my grand-babies, our family was beset with many traumas. Cancer tried to get its claws into several family members, our mum died (just old age) and tragically we had the sudden loss of my much loved twenty-year-old step-son in Scotland. For my partner, the devastation was even worse as he could not travel to Scotland to be with his family. We finally made it to the funeral but numbers were limited, supportive hugs were restrictive and masks were soaked in tears as we sobbed in a rainy cemetery. However many people lined the streets to say their goodbyes as the hearse made its way to the funeral. They stood scattered around the cemetery as we laid him to rest. At that time, we had no knowledge that the very politicians who were meant to be legislating for our safety, were brazenly ignoring every rule in the book.

Following his son's death, my partner's health nose-dived. He nearly lost his life to sepsis-pneumonia, then developed severe vomiting, devastating loss of balance and extensive and permanent hearing loss following the severe onset of Meniere's disease. Finally he developed acute psoriasis which his skin specialist feels is due to the bout of COVID-19 infection he had at Christmas 2021. The fear, frustrations and desperations throughout these times were compounded by being unable to receive appropriate, prompt care and accurate diagnosis. On top of this, was the fear of contracting COVID-19 every time he had to be admitted to hospital.

When he was suffering from the sepsis-pneumonia I spent several hours trying to get him the help I knew he needed. He was deteriorating before my eyes, initially misdiagnosed with COVID-19 infection and told to go home and isolate. I dread to think what the outcome would have been if, over the next few hours, I had not insisted on him getting further care, battling a system that was COVID-19 dominated. I shudder to think what was happening to others who did not have the confidence to fight. I knew how to argue his case but it was very stressful.

Luckily, neither of us contracted COVID-19 when Alpha and Delta were rife. But late December 2021, we fell prey to the Omicron strain. I was so unwell, that I will be forever thankful I had by then had three vaccines and that we had caught one of the milder strains. I can honestly say that I have never been so unwell in my life. This was made worse when shortly after that, I was diagnosed with Long Covid and a further onset of an acute virus again a few weeks later. Then came the news that I had anaemia, sticky blood and diabetes. Some of this was brought on by the steroids I had to take during the illnesses. I think I was maybe more seriously affected because in September 2021, I had been through major abdominal reconstructive surgery where I was predicted a 60% chance of complications post-operatively.

I made it back to work as soon as possible after the lateral flow tests became negative, but still felt like 'death warmed up.' However, as the breadwinner at that time and also because of my need to "make a difference", I felt obligated to getting on with it! I was incensed to hear a patient refusing to wear his mask as, according to him, COVID-19 "was a made-up disease designed to control the masses and we were stupid enough to fall for it".

Well here we are now in mid-2022 and although COVID-19 is still very much alive and kicking, we have all had to learn to live with it and the changes it has made to humanity. But I have decided to take a few lessons from this experience. For me, it has strengthened the importance of maximising time with family and friends, living each day to the best of our ability and not taking anything for granted. The trivia of life is exactly that. What matters is getting to hug those we love a little harder and longer when we get together. We won't let COVID-19 defeat our spirit.

Jabs and High Jinx
by Jill

Jill lives with her two cats, right on the edge of Greater London within five minutes' walk from the Kent countryside - the best of both worlds. She said that she is fortunate enough to have her family all close at hand, a job that can be carried out on Zoom, and mercifully no close contacts who have succumbed too badly to this potentially killer disease. "I had a good pandemic!"

January 2020

It was all very vague really. The news emerging from China was of a rather alarming illness that was affecting a large number of people in a place I'd never heard of. Very sad. Very remote.

One of my pupils, a lovely Chinese boy, was attending every Friday evening for his hourly tutorial. His mother, who had spent the Christmas holidays visiting relatives back home in China, had now returned and was complaining about not feeling well. I urged her to ensure that she went to the doctor and I had a fleeting thought about the virus that everyone was talking about. Of course I immediately dismissed that thought - after all China is a huge country!

February 2020

Apparently the virus now had a name – COVID-19 or a Coronavirus - never heard of it, although I must have rubbed shoulders with it on countless occasions previously, when I had caught a cold! The rumour was that Italy had now fallen victim to its effects and hospitals were struggling to cope. Not good to hear at all, but easily forgotten in the immediacy of our own lives maybe.

February is so often a grey, biting cold month, but this year I had plenty of great activities going on to keep me busy. I was enjoying my regular country walks with my sister Caroline, or with friends. I had regular yoga and Zumba classes at the local leisure centre. I child-minded my two-year-old granddaughter Francesca, every Friday, including taking her swimming and then immersing ourselves in the delights of a very lively playgroup. I was tutoring children every day at home in English and maths. I was helping out my local amateur dramatic group with coffees at our February performances. I had adopted two adorable kittens from Foal Farm, our local animal sanctuary. I had holidays booked up for the year in India, Italy and Scotland.

This month also saw Caroline and I enjoying the fantastic Illegal Eagles at the Churchill Theatre in Bromley, and two weeks later, we were at the Palladium, London to experience the brilliant Musical Box (an excellent early Genesis tribute band).

Life was good. I felt that, generally, things had calmed down a lot since the nightmare of 2017/2018 when my brothers, sister and I cared for Mum at home until her sad death at the age of ninety-four. Just days later, we then decamped from Mum's to my lovely brother, Mick's home. He had only weeks left to live, having received a devastating terminal diagnosis of pancreatic cancer. We nursed him at home throughout his last days. Mick died four days after Mum's funeral. It was awful. I had found the experience of watching a beloved brother being eaten away by this hellish disease utterly traumatic!

But now, life was for living and full of promise....

March 2020

The first Saturday evening in March found me with friends Pat and Lyn. I can recall demanding of them, "Why aren't we locking down, closing our borders, like the rest of Europe?" But the UK seemed to be dragging its heels before taking action against this new virus.

Less than two weeks into March, I had a strange week. It was my turn to cook a meal on Sunday evening for my daughter Emma, son-in-law James and son Ben. I had prepared a hot spicy chilli the day before, as that is how we like it. I was somewhat embarrassed to discover that in fact, it tasted really bland and not particularly enjoyable at all. Another culinary failure!! The next day I felt a bit off - not ill, just slightly lightheaded and lethargic.

For the rest of the week, I noted a lack of energy, but valiantly attended my Wednesday yoga class. However, on Thursday, I just did not fancy throwing myself around at Zumba and for the first time, cancelled my booking and instead fell asleep on the sofa. When Friday arrived, I was back to taking Francesca swimming, followed by the playgroup. We'd been there an hour or so, when Francesca came to tell me that she'd done a poo! Off to the loo we went, to change her nappy. Passing a young mum, she smiled and laughed, "Oh, it was you, smelling the place out!" I hadn't smelt a thing!

It must have been a month or two later before loss of taste and smell was recognised as a symptom of COVID-19. And so I realised that I had inadvertently become a "super-spreader" for that week in early March.... I also realised that I had been incredibly lucky to have experienced such a mild reaction.

I think my sister, Caroline became ill at the same time that lockdown was eventually imposed on the country on 23rd March. She really had quite a hard time with severe headaches, aching limbs and fluctuating temperatures over three weeks. I texted her daily for a health update, asking, " How is your breathing? Are your lungs ok?" Fortunately, she escaped these more dangerous and worrying symptoms - and her husband and son avoided catching COVID-19 altogether, despite sharing a house with her. They periodically placed a tray of food outside her bedroom, and then made a dash for it before she opened the door.

Of course this was well before there was any way of testing for the virus, but her symptoms so clearly matched those suffered by the 4000 new cases being reported every day, that we knew that Caroline had become another (unrecorded) statistic. In fact, in those early months, there must have been thousands of undiagnosed incidents of COVID-19. I have always believed that our actual daily figures were well underestimated then.

April 2020

So, lockdown began….

Rather strangely and quite inappropriately, I found myself regarding the whole thing with a slight tinge of excitement - like going into battle, I suppose. It was quite evident to me that, unlike so many other people, I benefitted from having a house to myself, a sizeable garden, easy access to open spaces for walking, and a regular financial income from a small pension.

My Friday child-minding of Francesca had come to an abrupt halt (grandparents not allowed!) I so much pitied those poor parents who had to battle working at home with their toddlers wreaking havoc in the home, and schoolchildren needing supervising with home learning. My own private tuition sessions had stopped too, but I quite welcomed the break! Then, my son Ben contacted me to suggest that he move in with me for the duration, as he too, was on his own in his little flat in Bromley.

Ben's first evening was interesting. He had decided to brave the germs in Sainsbury's and get some provisions in. There were recommendations for wearing masks now, to prevent contagion in all public places. Unsurprisingly, Ben had not yet had a chance to buy any, so ever resourceful, he set off with a pair of black (clean) underpants wrapped around his mouth and chin!

Anxious to keep fit and healthy at all costs, I quickly fell into a daily routine. A session of online yoga with Ben, then when he went upstairs to the study for work, I started a gruelling half hour workout with Joe Wickes. Taking advantage of the unusually good weather in 2020, I would venture into the garden, and then go for a walk over the common. Late afternoon, I would sit down to watch the daily bulletin on TV, updating us on the numbers of new cases of COVID-19 (including Boris Johnson!) with the dreadful death toll, regularly totalling over a thousand per day. The TV images in the UK and across the world were grim.

It must have been about this time that I was notified that my planned holidays for 2020 were now off the menu. A little dispiriting but in the whole scheme of things, it was very predictable. No problem - we'll simply postpone them until next year (we naively believed then!)

Morale was no doubt plummeting throughout the country, but a little cheer went a long way, and this arrived in the form of clapping the NHS on Thursday evenings. Feeling somewhat foolish on the first Thursday, I tentatively stood on my driveway with a collection of cymbals and tambourines. On the dot of eight o'clock, I began to rattle and clank, thinking I would be the only one. To my delight, a couple of neighbours came out, and then further down the road, a cacophony of random sounds blasted towards us, as more and more people showed their appreciation to all those working tirelessly in hospitals and care establishments. Through the racket, we also discerned the unmistakeable tones of the bagpipes wailing from number 56! Thus, the Thursday night ritual was established.

May 2020

What would we have done without Zoom?

It wasn't long before we realised that lockdown was not simply going to be a brief episode lasting a couple of weeks, as I had first of all imagined. We were really having to "socially isolate" (new expression) for the long term. I, like so many others, discovered the magic of Zoom. How fantastic it was to be able to chat online to my family and not miss out completely on Francesca's precious steps of growing up! Evenings were spent, exchanging news (not much) on iPads and laptops with friends, all of us shouting and talking over each other, or else being suddenly blanked out altogether. I found myself chatting much more frequently with friends than I would have normally done!

It was important to keep our minds busy, as well as our bodies, so we set ourselves daft challenges to be unveiled at the next Zoom meeting. I was very proud of my artistic pop up card, depicting a bright orange Donald Trump grasping a syringe of bleach in his hand. We also dressed up as characters in paintings, and attempted to recreate pictorial scenes. I guess we must have had some poetry in there somewhere too.

The weather was glorious. Was it a weird sort of compensation for all the misery that thousands of families must have been experiencing at this time? No compensation for many families, I'm sure!

The 8th May was no different. The day dawned warm and dry with a clear blue sky. This was when we celebrated VE day with a lockdown street party, spaced out in our front gardens with red, white and blue costumes and decorations, sandwiches, cakes and Prosecco. It was an extremely enjoyable day, walking round the street, and chatting at a distance to neighbours I had never seen before! A real sense of "community "was felt by all the residents, I think.

On the other hand, I lost my live-in lodger that month, as Ben decided to return home to his flat. He had struggled on valiantly to work with my intermittent Wi-Fi, but decided that his Bromley home offered a superior service to mine in West Wickham! Ironically, it was shortly after he left, that my Internet provider finally diagnosed the reason for my broadband languishing at about 3mb and restored it to 100mb. This had taken hours and hours of texts, problem reporting, phone calls and three home visits!

June 2020

It was during this month that the "rule of six" was permitted outside, which meant that I could meet up with friends for walks. This is something that we did regularly, taking advantage of the good weather that seemed to be a feature of this summer. My garden had benefitted somewhat from lockdown and looked rather colourful and lush. Eager to show off my horticultural efforts, I hosted a few mini gatherings at home in the hot sunshine.

My child-minding duties had resumed, as grandparents were now permitted to see their grandchildren. My daughter and son-in-law were mightily relieved to be able to work peacefully at home without a demanding two-year-old pestering them constantly. I have photos of Francesca splashing about happily in my back garden in her paddling pool.

Summer was definitely here!

July and August 2020

By this time, there was a feeling of optimism, at least in this part of the UK, that the crisis was on the decline. I started taking up where I had left off with my tutoring - but for the first time, online. Again, Zoom proved itself to be a very useful tool and, apart from occasional frozen screens or silent gesticulations, I was back in business.

The new cases of COVID-19 being reported in Bromley were now negligible, and although there were dire warnings daily from Chris Whitty and Jonathan Van-Tam that the pandemic was far from over, and that the winter would bring about a new surge, we felt a growing confidence that soon life would be back to normal. And what was more normal than being able to celebrate Francesca's third birthday in my daughter's garden? Pass the Parcel, birthday cake and presents galore, again in warm sunshine.

Long, hot walks along the River Medway in Kent, lunches with friends and trips into the countryside were enjoyed. You could stay overnight in a different household, and groups of six could gather outside long into the warm evening. The COVID-19 restrictions in these summer months didn't really appear to impact too much on our social lives. We travelled into Sussex to spend a day at the Weald and Downland Museum. We tackled the Go Ape experience at Leeds Castle. And now the idea of planning a holiday started to grow!

I should, at this point, emphasise that this is an account of my personal experience of the pandemic. I was very aware of my own very fortunate set of circumstances and knew that elsewhere, there were stories of tragedy, deprivation, misery and hardship.

September and October 2020

As summer drifted into autumn, the good weather continued, and so did our positive mood. Caroline and I spent a week on the border of Wales and Shropshire exploring the beautiful hills there.

Two weeks later we were off to Keswick in the Lake District with our two sons, Ben and Kenny. Our only regret was that Emma, James and Francesca were unable to join us as we had hoped. We would have totalled seven holidaymakers, and the "rule of six" was still being upheld. Even though the seventh was merely a small three-year-old, we didn't want to flout the rules! It is a very unusual sight to look down on Derwent Water from Catbells or climb Haystacks in warm sunshine (at least in my experience), and I have photos to witness the bright blue cloudless skies. There was only one day we returned to our holiday home soaked to the skin! Everything felt very "normal", our only concession to COVID-19 being the wearing of masks in shops and pubs. Having said that, the news was that the virus was beginning to spread again.

November 2020

New COVID-19 restrictions came into effect at the beginning of the month as case numbers were rising rapidly again across the whole of the UK. These involved reducing our contact with other people, and would remain in place until December 2nd (no doubt, to try and save Christmas!).

November is Pancreatic Cancer Awareness Month. I had recently heard that a good friend of mine had been diagnosed with this awful illness. It was the same cruel disease that had stolen my brother from me almost three years previously. I was challenged, along with some friends, to help in raising money for the charity. Despite the impact of COVID-19 across the world, other illnesses did not go away, and continued to deserve our attention. My calendar for this month was littered with walks, walks and more walks. According to my FitBit, I walked over two hundred and sixty miles in four weeks, and friends generously donated to my fund raising.

During November, having been sucked into our Street Christmas Lights Committee, I also found myself helping with securing glittery wreaths and lights to all the trees in the road. This was with a view to having a "switch-on" event at the end of the month. We distributed flyers to our neighbours, asking if a special effort could be made this particular year in decorating our houses. 2020 had been a difficult year for many people, and we felt that brightening up the street might bring a little boost as winter approached. So, on the last Sunday at five o'clock promptly, all the street residents came out to simultaneously turn on the lights on their designated trees, as well as illuminating their own homes. And very pretty it looked too - well worth the effort!

December 2020

A week later, we (the street committee) had planned an afternoon of Christmas festivities for our little community. The event itself was great! We had mulled wine and a food van. My musical next door neighbours played carols in their little band; DJ Val provided music from his front garden. We delivered poinsettias to the more elderly or vulnerable residents; Father Christmas presented the children with gifts. I ran a cake stall for the Pancreatic Cancer Charity; others had stalls for our local hospice, and guide dogs. There was a raffle. And all this was managed with social distancing - we were mindful that COVID-19 was no respecter of Christmas celebrations.

All in all, it was a great success. I was delighted to find that with my November walking and the cake stall, I was able to donate over £1100 to the Pancreatic Cancer Charity. So many of our residents had responded with great enthusiasm and enjoyment, and it was wonderful to meet, at a distance of course, neighbours I never knew existed.

During this time, we were under the impression that COVID-19 restrictions would permit us to meet up with family and friends for Christmas Day. Various announcements were made at the beginning of the month, refining and modifying "tiers", designed to reduce and keep "R below 1". However, the data showed the virus again increasing rapidly, and on 19th December 2020, the news that many people must have been disappointed to hear, was delivered. Because the situation had deteriorated, plans for Christmas and the New Year with friends and families, had to be scrapped. Those living in Tier 4 (which we were) were no longer allowed to mix with anyone outside their own household "bubble". This must have been a huge blow to so many!

Personally, I felt a little deflated, as I knew I would not be able to spend time with my son, daughter and granddaughter. Nevertheless, I had for some time, been included in the bubble of my sister's household, which meant that we would be a little party of four on Christmas Day. Modern technology also meant that I was able to watch Francesca excitedly tearing into her presents, on Zoom. I certainly could not feel particularly deprived. Perhaps the new restrictions were well founded, as shortly after Christmas, my children and Emma's in-laws all tested positive! I'm glad to say, that none of them were severely affected and made a rapid recovery.

And so the end of 2020 loomed.

For thousands, perhaps millions of people over the globe, the year had brought enormous tragedy, illness, anxiety, poverty, disappointment and loneliness. It will be a year that I suspect will have some historical significance - 2020, The Coronavirus Year!

As for me, I escaped virtually all of the more negative aspects of the pandemic. I count myself as extremely fortunate. Ironically, I remember 2020 as a year of warm sunshine, enjoyable experiences, close friendships, plenty of exercise and discovering a "community spirit" within my own neighbourhood.

In the meantime, 2021 was about to begin." It's going to be a much better year!" was something I heard relentlessly. And maybe it was going to be just that - the advent of a miracle cure-all, game-changing vaccine was just around the corner....

It would be a lie to say that I entered the year 2021 with a feeling of great optimism and joy. Winter is never my favourite season at the best of times, and now we were in the advent of another lockdown. On 4th January, due to drastic jumps in COVID-19 hospitalisations, we were once again instructed to "stay at home, protect the NHS and save lives". According to the never-ending statistics, the previous year's peak of patients being admitted to hospital had been surpassed by forty per cent. This lockdown lacked any novelty value that the first had, it was just tedious. And grey. And cold. And I had my tax return to complete.

Jabbed!

So, the walks continued, the Zoom sessions with friends continued, my tutoring online continued.... I think the only aspect of January that caused any break in my routine was a flurry of snow that lasted all of two days. It allowed Francesca to build her first snowman, a small mound of snow and mud with a couple of sticks, was the best that could be accomplished!

Nonetheless, a beacon of medical light was on the horizon. Ninety-one- year-old Margaret Keenan had received the first UK COVID-19 vaccine in December, followed shorty afterwards by a gentleman, rather bizarrely called William Shakespeare. It seemed that all my friends and acquaintances just could not wait to get that needle stabbed into their arms. Some went to great lengths, phoning their doctors' surgeries, clinics and hospitals regularly, with some even being rewarded with the longed-for appointment. There were online sites where you could calculate the date of your own expected appointment according to your age, general health and personal circumstances. "When is your jab?" was the question on everyone's lips.

Soon enough in mid-February, the message appeared on my phone asking me to attend Shirley Baptist Church the next week. The day dawned clear and bright, but bitterly cold and icy. Ever punctual, I arrived a couple of minutes early to find a very long queue of equally enthusiastic "jabees" standing outside. It was wonderful to see the "Great British Public" respond in such large numbers to the vaccine call - just NOT when I wanted to get inside, in the warm. It seemed an age before I reached the door, by which time I had decided that I was much more likely to die of pneumonia and hypothermia than COVID-19!

Inside the church hall, there was a very buoyant atmosphere with cheerful smiling volunteers and calm, serene nurses. People were stoically taking off coats and pulling up their sleeves and bracing themselves for the injection of precious vaccine. It was all over in a flash, but before I could make my escape, I was directed into the main church building with instructions to sit quietly for fifteen minutes. I suppose they had to ensure that no one had an unexpected reaction to the jab.

No one did that I could see, though we were subjected to a musical background of Chubby Checker singing "Let's Twist Again" and Cliff Richard's "Summer Holiday". Perhaps they assumed that people of my generation would appreciate those hits from the sixties. I bet "Needles and Pins" by the Searchers would have been there somewhere too! To distract myself, I found myself staring at the central cross on the altar. Rather oddly, it was decorated with a sign proudly proclaiming "LOVE WINE". I agreed wholeheartedly. It must have been quite a while before I realised that the final "E" was actually intended to be an "S". The floral script had thrown me completely! LOVE WINE/ LOVE WINS - nice sentiment either way....

Oh, and I didn't go down with pneumonia, hypothermia or COVID-19. I just had a very slightly tender arm for about a day. Lucky me again.

Vocabulary

During the following months, I was to revisit the wine-loving Church Hall twice more, to emerge as a fully vaccinated resident of the UK. How fortunate we were, that (by design, or by lucky accident) we were a country with a really robust vaccination programme, and a population generally willing to accept this course of action. Just as well, because a new word was entering our vocabulary. "Delta" was now the new predominant variant of the COVID-19, and no doubt responsible for the rapid growth in COVID-19 cases until the end of July.

Francesca, now three years old, was quickly developing an extensive vocabulary, but it was a reflection of these strange times that words like "hand gel, "mask" and "sanitise" seemed to be a perfectly normal part of her conversation. For the rest of us, "shielding," "self-isolating" and "social distancing" took on a particular significance - they were all commonly used in "the new normal". And what a shame, in this new normal, that our youngsters were growing up unable to read strangers' facial expressions - eyes only being visible!

Working from Home

As for our teenagers and young people, the pandemic must have been hugely limiting with a severe impact on the mental health of so many, when they should have been out having fun and mixing. My daughter, Emma, was very disgruntled when she was instructed to work from home, yet again. She really missed the buzz of working up in London, putting on her smart work clothes and high heels and socialising after work. At least she had a husband and daughter at home to keep her sane.

My son, Ben was more affected. He lived alone in a small, dark, one-bedroom flat and spent hour after hour staring at his work screen without moving. It must have been so frustrating to effectively and efficiently communicate with his team at a distance and finding his workload piling up incessantly. Consequently, his stress levels were going through the roof. Every week, I would drag him away from various investment and financial concerns and walk around the local park during his lunch hour to give his spine, his eyes and brain, a break. Eventually, later in the year, he took the difficult decision of handing in his resignation and taking some time out. He is now backpacking through Central America, from Mexico to Nicaragua. (Maybe it wasn't such a difficult decision after all.)

Holidays

An additional frustration of the early part of this year, was the realisation that, like an echo of last year, holiday bookings for 2020 and then 2021 had to be scrapped again. Well, not scrapped exactly, but a week in April in the Lake District with the family was postponed until October. Spending Easter with friends was cancelled (again!) A break, in Northumberland with friends, was rearranged for the second time. My intention to walk the West Highland Way in May with my sister was rolled over for a year (again!) and our holiday exploring the Italian Dolomites in July was also rolled over for a year (again!). I was beginning to think I would be too old to walk before I fulfilled these ambitions!

In actual fact, I don't remember feeling particularly surprised or upset at putting off my holidays for the second year. Ever the optimist, I felt confident that we'd eventually accomplish our plans, even if it might be some indefinable time later in the decade. In reality, I believed that the UK would be quite adequate for any breaks, just as soon as the latest COVID-19 restrictions would allow. And that is exactly what happened. Consequently I managed some wonderful weeks in the Peak District, Wales, Northumberland, Scotland and Cumbria. What was equally wonderful, was that somehow we managed to pick the few weeks it wasn't pouring with rain. Nothing to complain about!

Rain

Just as I envisage 2020 with wall-to-wall sunshine, this following year failed to be so generous, and it seemed that mud and drizzle were ever present. As the summer months crept towards us, the pandemic statistics improved and a greater sense of freedom loomed, but unfortunately so did the rain clouds. Umbrellas and raincoats became essential items to accompany any visit or event.

At the end of May, along with the Keswick/Windermere Road Committee I had planned a repeat of the "Tea in Front Gardens" celebration that had been so successful for VE Day last year. This year, unfortunately, it was a wash out. " A few soggy cakes under a gazebo" would have been a better name for the occasion.

Similarly, for the August Bank Holiday, we had organised a Grand Street Party with food vans, children's games, fund-raising stalls and bunting. It didn't actually rain (much) but dark grey clouds cast a very dusky pall over the whole day. Temperatures felt definitely well below average, even for the UK! A few brave souls emerged stoically out of their houses and we sat, under blankets, in a miserable little huddle in the middle of the road for a couple of hours before thankfully scuttling back into the relative warmth of home.

Scarecrows

On the bright side, an idea that I'd had for some time after a visit to Kettlewell a few years previously, came to fruition.

Kettlewell is a pretty village in Yorkshire, fairly unremarkable, except for its fantastic annual scarecrow festival. I had timidly suggested emulating this event in our own roads some time ago, and my suggestion had completely fallen on deaf ears. However, the pandemic had brought our community together in a way I had never witnessed before. Our WhatsApp was now a thriving hub of news, jokes, advice, exchanges... and now ... the plans for our very own scarecrow festival.

It was a great success. Our creative residents responded with such imagination and humour, producing in their front gardens, the weird and wonderful, the creepy and the hilarious. My own effort was a slightly disrespectful nod to our hallowed NHS. I'd constructed a rather scruffy nurse, seated in a chair, surrounded by wine bottles. It was hugely gratifying to discover that the word had spread around the area, so we devised a scarecrow trail for parents and children to follow during the summer holidays. I so loved to hear the sound of young voices laughing and exclaiming as they passed my garden. Something to repeat next year, I think!

And now

Other world events are now dominating the airways. Our media is no longer announcing the latest statistics for hospitalisations or for the next raft of rules and restrictions. The general attitude to the virus goes down the lines of, "Don't particularly want to catch it but it probably won't feel much more than a slight cold". Whether that is a sensible outlook or not, it clearly reflects the fact that COVID-19 has lost its sting, and we, consequently, have lost our fear (and possibly our masks too?).

On the positive side, it's been uplifting to see how scientists from all over the world can collaborate in finding defences against killer diseases. People will rise above the difficulties that nature can throw at them. Those involved in care will toil tirelessly under the most gruelling circumstances. On a local level, I have been delighted to discover a feeling of involvement in my community and acquaint myself with those erstwhile strangers who live on my doorstep.

In conclusion, I can only say that I had a "good" pandemic, without any of the drama, distress, sickness or hardship suffered by much of the world population. I've certainly had thoroughly miserable episodes in my life, but the events of 2020/2021 were absolutely nothing more than a bit of an inconvenience.

Nevertheless, I hope I will never take my good fortune for granted. Being aware of the advantages my life has, through nothing more than luck is something I should always appreciate. As this dreadful global occurrence has shown us, you never know what is round the corner...

Pandemic challenges: working on the frontline
by Jackie

Jackie lives in North Vancouver and works in a retail pharmacy. She has been a frontline worker throughout the pandemic. Her two daughters, their partners and her granddaughter also live in the area.

It was March 2020 and I had a trip booked to Vietnam. COVID-19 was becoming a reality and suddenly travel did not seem like a sensible idea. The borders were closing between countries in Asia and I did not want to find myself trapped in a foreign country unable to get home. Instead I decided go to Cuba with my friend and her husband. There were no cases of COVID-19 in Cuba and this seemed like a safe option.

Once in Cuba, due to restricted Wi-Fi, we were not fully aware of just how the crisis was escalating across the world. However, during the week, the situation began to ramp up significantly. My daughters back home in Canada were quite alarmed. They informed me that Prime Minister, Trudeau, had stated that Canada would be closing its borders soon and it was time for Canadians to come home. At this stage we started to become concerned as to whether our flight would leave Cuba, but thankfully it took off as scheduled. Landing in Toronto was a very good feeling and all the passengers cheered as we touched down on Canadian soil.

My manager had contacted me to let me know that protocols had been laid down for citizens returning to Canada and that there was now a requirement to quarantine for fourteen days. Quarantine was manageable. I went out for lots of walks and read books. My daughter and her boyfriend live with me so we occupied different areas of the house and had no contact. They picked up my groceries, as I didn't go into the supermarkets. There was panic buying at this time and many food items and toilet paper were in short supply. I prepared food whilst they were at work and religiously cleaned the kitchen after using it so it was sanitized and ready for them to use when they returned home. While I was in quarantine, my staff kept me informed. I was aware that at work all hell was breaking loose and it was busy on an unprecedented level.

After the fourteen days of quarantine, I returned to work and it was indeed overwhelming. Doctors were working remotely and had closed their offices. People were panicking as they couldn't easily get in contact with their physicians and were concerned about getting their medication. The College of Pharmacists of British Columbia were quick to respond to the crisis and immediately enforced bylaws. These gave pharmacists sweeping prescribing powers, including narcotics, to ensure we could meet our patients' needs. The result was that pharmacists were now prescribing for patients and dispensing their medication, significantly increasing our workload.

We did feel exposed dealing directly with the public and we had to wear full Personal Protective Equipment (PPE) all day long, which was extremely uncomfortable. When I returned home at the end of a working day, I would wipe down all surfaces I touched and then shower and wash all of my clothes. It was a time consuming process which made a long day even longer.

Whilst work was difficult and stressful, the appreciation shown to us by the public made it all worthwhile. People daily verbalized how grateful they were that we showed up each and every day to help them and do our jobs, despite the difficult circumstances. At 6pm every evening, the public came outside and clapped and cheered for all the front-line workers. This really helped carry us through those difficult times.

At this time we were only allowed to meet with people in our immediate household. Technically, we should not have seen my other daughter and her husband as they were living in a different household. However, we chose to break that rule and form a bubble with them as my daughter was in the late stages of pregnancy and needed the support from her sister and myself.

In December 2020, my first granddaughter was born. We were not allowed to go to the hospital to visit them, but we met her when they came home when the baby was two days old. We all wore masks when visiting, as we were so worried about potentially exposing a newborn to the virus.

As 2021 began, we were hopeful that things would improve and that this would all come to an end. However, this was not the case and again all travel plans had to be cancelled. A trip to India in March and also Portugal in the summer did not come to fruition and my daughter's boyfriend's parents had to cancel a trip to Canada to visit their son.

We all welcomed the approval of the vaccine in 2021, hoping that this would be the means to the end of this pandemic. The roll out of the vaccine, however, was not well orchestrated. The provincial government and the British Columbia Pharmacy Association did not communicate effectively with pharmacies, the very people who would take on the added task of administering the vaccine. They released statements without consultation, advising the public to contact their pharmacy to get vaccinated. This resulted in hundreds of phone calls and in one day we received over three hundred phone calls, which severely impacted our workflow. So, once again, we were immersed in a chaotic working environment, which could have been avoided through more effective communication.

It was around this time that we began to notice a shift in attitude. From being appreciated and supported in our efforts to help the public and play a role in getting through this crisis, now the anti-maskers and anti-vaxxers began to emerge and create a negative atmosphere. It was very disillusioning to follow social media and read the misinformation being spread and to read of all the protests and attacks by these people. What was being perpetrated on these platforms was not just a difference of opinion, but a level of thinking that, to me, just did not make sense and that no rational person could support or understand.

Finally, at this stage of the pandemic, I do feel burnt out and exhausted from just trying to keep up with continuously evolving protocols. Every day there are changes and new directives that have to be followed and passed onto our public. What was relevant yesterday is obsolete today.

We are now also involved in administering booster doses and supplying rapid antigen tests to the public. This is all on top of our normal workload. However I am cognisant that I'm lucky to have been employed throughout this pandemic. I have not been financially impacted and have been able to spend time with those who mean the most to me, my family. I have not lost my livelihood, my loved ones or my life to this virus which is NOT "just a cold".

It feels as if life is finally getting back to normal now. I see friends and go out for dinner and to events. I've made travel plans and I'm optimistic that this nightmare is coming to an end. I still try to wear a mask in public and socially distance, as it makes sense to take precautions wherever possible. Work is still too busy, but it does feel like normality is returning.

I look back on this and realize this has been a historic event to live through. I have been disillusioned with some of society's response to the COVID-19 pandemic, but I'm grateful that I've been fortunate and I'm proud that I've done my part to step up and help wherever possible during this crisis.

Therapeutic Musings
by Emma

Emma lives in Norwich in the UK. She is a therapist, education consultant and a foster carer.

COVID-19 crept up on me, on the edges of my awareness. It was something happening elsewhere in the world and wasn't worth paying too much attention to. The media had made a fuss about SARS a few years earlier and that had come to nothing. This was obviously media nonsense again.

Let me put some context around this. I had other stuff going on in my life. My elderly father had died on Valentine's Day 2020 and I was coming to terms with the first loss of a parent. I was running a rapidly expanding therapy and education consultancy business, the result of a career change a few years earlier. I'd left a twenty-five year career in education, working as both a teacher and an advisor after retraining as a therapist. Additionally, we had become foster carers, something my husband and I had wanted to do for years. After Dad died, we were wrestling with whether we could continue fostering. Our last placement had finished in January 2020 and my business was expanding rapidly and taking more and more of my time and energy. It was also clear that my mum was going to need some support too, as she adjusted to life on her own.

I have no recollection of hearing about COVID-19 prior to my dad's funeral on March 3rd 2020. He was well known locally and his funeral was well attended, as was the wake at our local pub afterwards. Celebrating my dad's life in this way was comforting and something I absolutely expected to be able to do. Within a few short weeks I would come to realise just what a privilege it was to have been able to do this. As a family, we soon became grateful that Dad had passed when he did. He had breathing and heart issues and whilst we realistically knew he wouldn't see 2020 out, we weren't expecting him to go quite as early as February. The feeling of having been cheated of a bit more time with him was rapidly replaced by a sense of relief that he had died peacefully in his own bed at home. He would have struggled with all the restrictions and would have surely succumbed, had he caught it and who knows where or how he would have died. The haunting images on the news of what was happening in ICUs reinforced this daily.

My memories of the week or two running up to the first lockdown are limited. I remember reassuring a young client who expressed anxiety about the situation, by explaining about the SARS scares that had never come to anything. I did apologise afterwards. The numbers of pupils in the school where I worked as a therapist two days a week were rapidly dwindling. We had dinner with friends in a Turkish restaurant the weekend before the lockdown started as we were planning to go to Turkey together in June 2020. We laughed, convinced it would all be over in a couple of weeks and joked about whether we should hug as we said our goodbyes at the end of the evening. We did. I also took my mother an old iPad and showed her how to FaceTime, just in case.

My next memory is of watching Boris Johnson on the news when he made the announcement that the country was going into lockdown. Both our adult sons had made the decision to spend the lockdown with us and the eldest had brought his girlfriend with him.

I have always been a fan of the dystopian television series, 'Black Mirror'. Possibly my most vivid memory of those first few weeks was sitting on the sofa thinking that somehow things were not real and that I was in an episode of the programme. Maybe I'd wake up and it would all be a bad dream? That sense of horror was to stay with me for many months, slowly fading as the pandemic progressed.

The sense of surrealness was underlined by the loss of routine. All my work dried up almost overnight. All five of us in the family were ill during the first week of lockdown with cold symptoms, whether it was COVID-19 or not we will never know. My younger sister stepped in, doing the shopping for both us and our mum. I vividly remember my sister FaceTiming me from the supermarket to check which particular product we wanted. After several days staying inside, it was strange to vicariously experience the outside world via a video call made from my local Tesco. Getting caught up in watching the 'Tiger King' on Netflix only added to the strangeness of it all!

I couldn't sit and do nothing, so the first few weeks of lockdown I tackled the spring cleaning. With the kids' help we cleared the loft and sheds and jet washed everything outside, repainted sheds and my summer house where I see clients. I wrote pieces about mental health for a local SEND charity, and FaceTimed and called friends and family members who were on their own. I kept in contact with clients offering advice and posted resources endlessly on my business Facebook page – the need to feel useful was strong.

My husband is a district and county councillor. He was incredibly busy from the very beginning, co-ordinating the relief efforts locally as well as being involved in the logistics of setting up temporary morgues and ensuring homeless people were off the streets. I made a sign that said 'Mission Control' which I put on his office door.

Like many of us, we FaceTimed: we kept in regular contact with my mum and my sister (both on their own), having family meals together on FaceTime. Saturday night became games night with our kids and there were moments of real fun. I can't imagine what it was like to be on your own during the lockdown, but as glad as I was to have my family with me, inevitably there were moments of tension too.

When it became apparent that the pandemic wasn't going away anytime soon, knowing there was a shortage of foster carers and having lost one income, the decision to take another fostering placement was obvious. Within a few days we welcomed a nearly eight-month-old baby boy into our lives. I'll call him Jack - obviously not his real name. He'd been badly neglected, was covered in eczema and what turned out to be scabies bites (we only realised this when we caught it!). He'd not been interacted with properly and it took a few days before we had any positive response from him. Having Jack and watching him develop was joyous. He was a positive focus for all of us and without normal work pressures we were able to spend hours with him, making up for lost time. Fostering normally involves taking a child to a contact centre to meet parents but everything had moved online. Fifteen minutes on a video call doesn't sound that long, but when it is with parents who don't know how engage with their child and you have a baby who is not in the least bit interested, it can really seem like an age!

To try to ensure he was interacting with people, even from a distance, we took Jack out daily in his pram. Like many others, we walked for an hour every day. People made lots of fuss about the Blitz spirit of lockdown. I'm not quite sure it was that, but people definitely took the time to say hello and smile and the village where I live was a friendlier place. "Clap for Carers" was a welcome excuse to go outside too and catch up with the neighbours. Whilst the village might have felt friendlier, going shopping was a scarier proposition. Back to my feeling of surrealism again, I vividly remember wandering around the supermarket, feeling wary and keeping my distance from people. I would wonder if this would be the trip when I would catch COVID-19.

I couldn't let my business fail, so I took the decision around May/June of 2020 to take the business online. Some therapists have offered online appointments for a long time, but it had never appealed to me. I will fully admit I was totally wrong about it. I picked up a whole new demographic of clients, young men in their teens and twenties who were clearly far more comfortable with communicating in this way. They didn't want to come in for face-to-face sessions when it was finally possible to do so.

So many aspects of life moved online, including my Friday morning Slimming World group (I actually lost weight in lockdown!) and my peer supervision group with fellow therapists. Lots of training companies put their training online at a reduced price and I took advantage of this. I have a mixture of online and face-to-face clients to this day.

Fast forward to today: May 2022. Jack was with us for ten months and moved to a new "forever family" with whom we are in touch, and we still see him regularly. His moving on was the hardest placement ending I've ever had. It is obvious that he was a huge distraction and the pandemic coming so quickly after my father's death meant I didn't really grieve until Jack left.

Our youngest son started university in September 2020, in London. A virtual Freshers' Week wasn't the normal experience but he settled in well, although he spent most of the year back at home with us in the subsequent lockdowns.

I went back into the high school in the autumn of 2020, where I worked therapeutically and had processes in place to ensure I could see my students via video call when the schools were shut down again in January 2021. This wasn't without its challenges. I'd tried working with some of my younger clients online when I started seeing clients again in the first lockdown. Keeping them engaged was far more challenging than doing it in person. I have so much respect for my teaching colleagues for whom this became the new normal. Even seeing my teens online had its moments: I have been upstaged by cats eating cheesecake; younger siblings; guided tours of houses and seeing things I'm sure parents probably didn't want me to see! The numbers in my private practice are currently at an all-time high with a waiting list and the numbers on my waiting list at school are equally high too. The severity of the issues I am seeing is noticeably worse, due to local mental health services being stretched more than ever. It is easy to say that kids are resilient and for many that is true but it is not the case for all. Many of my neurodivergent clients enjoyed not having to go to school but have had real struggles going back (some still ongoing) and those children for whom home was not a safe place suffered greatly. I also picked up adult clients who had experienced relationship issues or breakdowns during the pandemic. As I mentioned earlier, babies like Jack and very young children were impacted too, missing out on opportunities to socialise with others outside their immediate family and I am regularly hearing about young children with separation anxiety as a result.

This year (2022) has been busy for us socially. Lots of events are being held again and people have wanted to reconnect. It has been lovely but at the same time I'm not sure that I'm quite as gregarious as I was pre-COVID-19. Maybe it's age, who knows?

Whatever our experiences of the pandemic, one thing is true. We lived through a truly historic event. My kids joked that their grandkids would probably want to interview them about it for a homework project. My kids are fortunate enough to be able to say that they mostly sat on their backsides and watched Netflix and for that I will be eternally grateful.

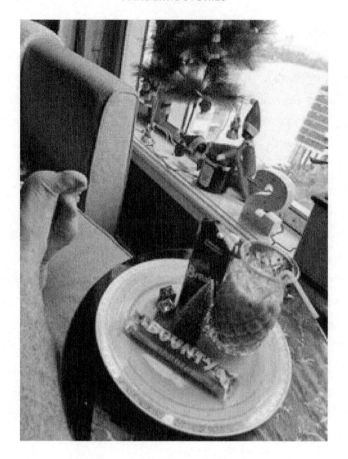

From Palace to Pandemic
by Darren

Aboriginal Australian single parent Darren: former teacher, chef and butler, now works as a palace manager in the Middle East. Travelled during the pandemic and survived.

So! Finally, the good ship COVID-19 cruised into the calm waters of the Middle East's Gulf and dropped anchor in the Kingdom of Bahrain. We all thought that it was just going to be one of those outbreaks that another country has, a bit like Ebola or a civil war or unrest that you see on the TV, "won't really affect us," we all said and "life goes on". That was back in 2020 and who knew that ship was never to leave, and we are now in 2022.

I have been one of the fortunate ones who have been able to travel, not only for work but also for pleasure, since this horrid virus kicked off. Being a healthy, good-looking, middle-aged male, triple Pfizer vaccinated and a pro-masker, so far I have managed to dodge the COVID-19 bullet and all other viruses as well. Apart from the reaction from the vaccine that saw me in bed each time for a minimum of twenty-four hours, life has been great for the most part and for the first time in years, I haven't actually had a cold or been unwell.

COVID-19 really started while I was on a recruitment drive in Kerala, India canvasing for hotel staff for the ruling royal family back in the Middle East. Then, life was carefree and travel was as easy as jumping on a plane with passport in hand and a credit card, when you could eat in public with more than four people per table, no masks or people getting sick by simply talking to each other or shaking hands.

Watching the CNN news in India between interviews and spa treatments, which was another thing that was soon to be a thing of the past, the reality of COVID-19 spreading to our Little Kingdom was becoming more and more of a reality. Talk of airports closing was imminent and I was due to leave India in a few days' time, just before Dubai's airport shut up shop. Luckily my ticket was via Oman on the way back to the Kingdom or I would have been stuck in the United Arab Emirates (UAE). The thought of a road trip by camel was not floating my boat at all. I was grateful that for the first time in twenty-two years I had not flown with Emirates, a blessing there.

Being one to think out of the box and a closet entrepreneur, I asked my driver to do a detour on the way back to the hotel via a few pharmacies to get as many masks as I could legally, knowing they were going to be in high demand with a possible shortage. Loaded up with as many as I could purchase, I headed home to Bahrain wearing my "super dooper, you beaut, all bells and whistles bright yellow duck beak mask, with filters on either side". I did not know that this was to be the norm for me for the next two years. Wearing masks everywhere was to become law in Bahrain with an on the spot fine of 20BD local currency if found NOT wearing one in public.

It was evident very early in the piece, that Bahrain was a leader with the way in which they dealt with COVID-19 testing and contact tracing. We never fully closed the airport and it remained open to everyone especially its citizens, unlike other countries. Airport testing and temporary medical facilities were erected instantly to deal with the sick and infected. Mobile drive-through testing stations were positioned around the country and testing was done on a mass scale. This was effective from the get-go, followed by a vaccination programme for its citizens and expat workers, which ran rings around other countries who were still scratching their heads. Our COVID-19 phone app system worked very well and was effective in keeping people up-to-date, safe and kept a track of their testing and vaccination records. Everyone followed the advice from the experts and less from Google and Facebook as people wore their masks daily and followed the rules. Lockdowns were put in place for a very short time and only supermarkets, hospitals and pharmacies and other essential businesses were allowed to open to the public. Enter the new age of takeaway food delivery, home schooling and dial-a-pet-groomer. All businesses suffered but the ones that did survive learned quickly how to restructure their operation to cope with the closures. If your business sold food, it was classed as an essential business which was a handy loophole and allowed many businesses to continue functioning. This started the mass introduction of pop-up food sections in shops and businesses that were completely not food-related but were then able to continue to operate. The government soon closed them down and changed the law again! A bit like COVID-19 really, changes happened daily and with little or no warning.

After the last lengthy lockdown, the island slowly began to reopen and relax its strict social distancing rules previously enforced that made it almost impossible for some businesses to operate normally. Gyms, pubs and clubs, salons and restaurants eventually fully opened but for vaccinated people only. Your "green vaccination shield" had to be visible upon entry. THEN enter the Omicron bus that crashed and spilled out its precious evil load, impossible to control. The infection rate went from as low as fifty-seven people to thousands in days. Thankfully most people got through the infection period without being ill at all, with most having little to no symptoms when tested positive, the result of being vaccinated? Let's hope!

As the manager of a large organization of over one hundred staff, we had been PCR testing weekly since the start and this could be as often as every second day. We were doing famously well with little to no cases at all until Omicron hit, with any infected staff being quickly shuffled off to a hotel on for between seven to fifteen days and then getting a "get out of jail pass" if negative.

COVID-19 wasn't so kind to a few close friends of mine, who caught it in the early stages before the vaccine was introduced. Notably a very dear friend, who contracted the virus, was placed on a respirator and died suddenly one morning after I had spoken to him only the night before. Begging me to help him move to a better facility, I assisted in the transfer to an upgraded hospital but this was to be short lived. Chatty as he was using text, he appeared to be ok and looked fine from his selfie, considering the circumstances, or at least as well as one could be when hooked up to a respirator. I went to bed, with the selfie picture he had sent me with my mind still in that hospital. My last words to him were, "Don't be silly, you idiot. You are not going to die! You will be ok, chat tomorrow." That tomorrow didn't come for him and my friend died the next morning of a heart attack, COVID-19 related. This not only ended his life abruptly but also our working relationship of over twenty-two years. It affected his events com   which had to close down and his passing put many p   out of work. The end of an era. R.I.P buddy x

In the height of the pandemic, sadly another work colleague's mother passed away from natural causes in the UK in the Lake District. As she had no immediate family, I jumped on a plane to the UK to help her settle up things and support her during this difficult time. The plane was empty and going through Customs in Heathrow took all but five minutes as I was the only one there when I arrived. Everything at the airport was closed and very few people were travelling at the time: it was literally like a ghost town. Not wanting to risk the chance of catching COVID-19, I avoided public transport and made arrangements for a driver to take me to the rolling hills of Cumbria in the Lake District. Unfortunately, the funeral service had to be held outside the quaint little country church due to the COVID-19 restrictions. As the pall bearer walked slowly towards us with the hearse following, we all stood along the fence line watching and getting wetter and wetter as the rain got heavier and heavier! Thank the Lord! The pastor spoke up and said, "The hell with the rules! If I don't let you guys IN this church, I will be burying you all next week from pneumonia". Forever grateful, we all scurried into the church with umbrellas flapping just before the coffin was carried in. The funeral carried on as it should have and of course we were all spaced out. Welcome to the birth of social distancing.

As we were right in the middle of the pandemic, we were able to travel around and do some sightseeing, without any tourists. The days were glorious and the weather held up for the remainder of my visit, minus the usual crowds that WOULD have been there at that time of the year and we were always guaranteed a parking space wherever we went.

Apart from the doom and the gloom, and being fortunate to be able to travel for work and pleasure despite lock downs and border closures, I went to the South of France again, work related of course! France had just opened up to vaccinated visitors after a strict lockdown and, if you had a valid reason for which to travel, you were allowed in. Upon arrival and loaded up with the required paperwork including vaccination and PCR test results, I was waved through without anyone actually checking the reams of requisite paperwork which was typical of most places, except for Australia! France did however introduce the "green shield" and the COVID-19 passport while I was there, which made it near impossible to enter most public places, restaurants, malls and so on. In my eyes there appeared to be no such thing as social distancing at all. Sidewalk cafes overflowed with Parisians sitting smoking and drinking their espressos and eating their croissants, and the shopping centres were full at this time. Life in France seemed quite normal. Viva la France!

Australia!! Let's discuss Australia! I was ashamed to be called an Australian up until then (2022.) Australia slammed its doors, shut up shop, pulled the blinds down and hung out the sign that read "NO ENTRY" to everyone including its own people. Aussies were desperately trying to get back to their home country and many hundreds were stranded, stuck and homeless and were forced to spend thousands of dollars on overpriced plane tickets. The obsession with keeping COVID-19 from lapping the golden sands of OZ, tight caps were implemented that made it impossible to get a seat on a plane back to the land of down-under Australia. Add to that the compulsory two-week hotel quarantine if you were one of the fortunate ones to get a seat, you would be allowed in, then locked up for the privilege and treated like a temporary prisoner.

Being a resident and having an overseas work visa that showed that I had been out of Australia for more than ninety days gave me a golden pass. After a long twenty-one hours of travel time, I arrived in Brisbane late at night, not knowing where I was staying until we landed but pleasantly surprised all the same when I got to the hotel. I was, maybe more than most, prepared for the ordeal, thanks to a few Facebook groups, which gave helpful hints and information. These gave first-hand accounts from previous and current travellers who had been incarcerated in their mother country by the government. Tips and tricks flooded the Internet on how to survive and get through the two-week lock up in a non-smoking room with a view if you were lucky and a window that was usually closed or locked with no balcony and no human contact. Then entered yet another change, the police and "Big Brother" watching every room on every floor. Stricter rules were implemented which incurred fines if broken.

Fortunately, the hotel that I was sent to was in the city and had a pleasant view of the river and the city street below. I sat here most days, gazing out or looking down at the people who appeared like ants, rushing around and entering the train station entrance, which resembled their nest bringing food, back for their queen. Apart from that, I sat at the window looking at people living in the high-rise apartments that surrounded me or just wondering what the weather was like on the outside, or the temperature other than mine in the room that was set on a steady twenty one degrees.

Food reviews seemed to be the main pastime, with many people posting almost immediately upon arrival if not daily, some good but mostly bad reviews about the food! No-one really enjoys eating out of a Styrofoam container and using plastic or wooden cutlery, even at a picnic, let alone three meals a day for two weeks. I was one of the blessed ones that had food supplied by the actual hotel itself, thank God. My food always arrived hot and fresh with a menu that changed daily, all of which I re-plated onto a china plate that I had been advised to bring. A great tip! I also brought cutlery, knife, cutting board, tall glass, coffee mug, paper napkins and place mats as well as a washing up sponge and tea towels. My meals were also complemented with the odd gift hamper that family and friends would send me. A very close friend who worked in the city a few doors down would send me treats most days. On two occasions, my son drove one hour each way to deliver a pie from a well-known and famous Pie House with an all time Aussie favourite, custard tart.

Another close friend sent a beautiful bunch of native wild flowers, local honey and handmade chocolates with activity packs for my already famously by now, ornately decorated room. Word had got around that the guy in Room 609 had redecorated and turned it into a Santa's grotto. Yes, I was locked in for Christmas Day and I would eventually get out on Boxing Day, which would be the new Christmas Day for me in 2021!

Apart from all of the festive stuff that kept me busy, my dance card was well and truly full from the minute I woke up until bed -time. Before I left the Middle East where I flew out from originally, I had been given fourteen small boxes from friends and they had numbered them. Each box was then filled with something nice for me to open each day, a kind of adult advent calendar for grown ups! My nativity scene was made up from whatever I could muster to represent all the figures. Christ was represented by an egg placed in a small bowl with straw made out of the brown paper bags, which the food arrived in three times a day. Animals were my chocolate stuffed dates, Joseph and Mary were suitably dressed around men's and ladies' perfumes (Christmas gifts I had with me) and the three wise men were the hotel's shampoo, conditioner and body lotion, that no one ever uses but takes home all the same. The rest of the time I was inventing gift-wrapping ideas using the brown paper bags that the food came in.

The rental bike I had hired was rarely used and sat there most days. My bathtub was full of disposable plastic containers and the paper bags were piled high. I had survived with the help of everyone including Facebook, which would fill in the time, along with long showers and the odd three-hour bubble bath using the dish washing liquid. The three meals a day always came around all too quickly and if there was ever a dead moment there was always the TV, Netflix or I simply called a friend and chatted for hours. Regular calls from various health and welfare services also filled in the time. The only human contact was being tested for COVID-19 by the nurses.

At 8am on the morning of Day Fifteen, which was Boxing Day, there was a knock at the door by the police. I was then escorted down in the lift with what seemed to be way more luggage then I had arrived with, barely room enough for me and the officer and all of my stuff. It was all very sterile and formal as I was let free out of the back service door of the hotel. I felt as if I was a cow that had been locked up all winter and this was the first day of spring being let out to greener pastures. My senses were overloaded with the scent of blossoms from the trees that lined the streets nearby. It was a Sunday AND it was Boxing Day morning so there was no city traffic at all and very little pollution. In fact, the sounds of people milling around and traffic were missing and it was just me and my luggage, sitting on the corner waiting for my son to arrive. Farewell Hotel California, in the words of the song "a lovely place", "such a lovely place." (NOT!)

Fast forward one year and we were heading towards Christmas 2021. Again, I managed to book another first-class ticket home to Australia. This year though, I only spent one week in the hotel, the second week I was let out to finish quarantine at home after meeting all the requirements. Christmas was on Christmas Day with the family and life was back to normal or as normal as it could be. At that point I still hadn't caught COVID-19 and I still had all of those masks from India…. but that's another story!

Let's Try for a baby!
by Danny

Danny, a record label executive based in South London, lives with his Swedish fiancée Amanda and their son Caspian who will forever be known as a "COVID-19 baby". At the beginning of the pandemic, they spent several months in Sweden.

As 2019 came to a close, Amanda and I couldn't have been further from one another. Geographically speaking I mean. I had spent my Christmas holidays on the east coast of Australia celebrating a close friend's wedding. Amanda was at her family home in Sweden singing songs and drinking Yulemust. It was hard being away from one another but we had a lot to look forward to. We had agreed that upon our return to the UK, Amanda was going to leave her rented accommodation in Haggerston, North-West London and move into my one-bed flat in Thornton Heath, South London.

We had both done a lot of thinking over Christmas and had mega plans for the year ahead. We stood to save a lot of money living together, both working well-paid full-time jobs, paying a single mortgage and splitting the bills. Whilst doing our best to enjoy ourselves, we had also discussed the idea of trying for a baby. We realised that this was a process and the chances were that it could take considerable time for Amanda to get pregnant. There were many unknowns.

The first half of the year was going to involve lots of eating, drinking and hopefully travelling. The next event in the social calendar was a "Noughty Boys" live gig at The Dogstar in Brixton at the end of January. (The Noughty Boys is the cover band I play in with my friends). Over two hundred and fifty people turned up and the event was a roaring success. My family met Amanda's family for the first time. The energy and excitement in the room was something I will never forget. Little did we know that this event was the last time we would be able to enjoy the company of our closest friends and family for some time to come. Ironically, we believe this was the night our baby was conceived.

Amanda had stopped taking the pill and we planned to carry on with life as normal whilst trying for a baby. Just five days later, I was working from home when I picked up my phone to see I had six missed calls from Amanda. She never calls. The phone rang again for a seventh time.... I heard three shaky words from the other end of the phone. 'Danny... I'm pregnant'.

We were both in shock and we certainly digested the news in our own way. Even though we had agreed to try, it was still a total shock that it had happened so quickly. We had nine months to get ourselves set. If all went to plan we were going to welcome a child into the world in late October 2020.

COVID-19 had first hit my consciousness in mid-December. We had heard a few murmurs on the news. It was 'contained' in a localized area of China... No cause for concern. January 2020, we were both more aware of the 'virus' but were still very relaxed about the situation. The seriousness of COVID-19 seemed to coincide with our big news. Italy had gone into lockdown and we were told the UK was just a few weeks behind. In the second week of March, Boris Johnson announced that measures would be implemented to try and contain the virus spreading across the UK.

We suddenly had to make some very difficult decisions regarding what to do and where to go. London had particularly high infection rates and we just did not know how dangerous such a hitherto unknown virus could be for a pregnant woman. Amanda could no longer go to work, as her job involves close contact with the public. Suddenly she was pregnant, jobless and frightened about her and our baby's health and safety. Amanda had many long conversations with her family who said we were more than welcome to stay with them in Sweden for a few weeks whilst everything calmed down. They live in a very remote part of the country and close contact is almost non-existent. Sweden had taken a very different approach to COVID-19. Low spread, no restrictions and the economy was steady. Due to the nature of my job, with a phone and a computer, I can just about work from anywhere. Whilst this seemed like an obvious choice, we were very aware that by leaving the country, we would miss our scheduled pregnancy appointments at the hospital. If anything was to happen to any of our friends or family whilst we were away, we probably wouldn't be able to get home very easily.

We had three options and a massive decision to make.

1). Stay in South London in our one bed flat
2). Head back to Norwich to stay at my mum's house

3). Travel to Sweden and wait for things to calm down.

We booked a single outbound flight to Gothenburg. No return.

Our ten weeks in Sweden involved a lot of walking, talking and Zoom calls. Looking back it was a quiet and uneventful period in our lives. Whilst people were being told to stay at home to save lives, COVID-19 never really 'arrived' in Sundsandvik. Amanda was suffering with nearly all of the symptoms one can suffer from. She spent a lot of time in bed. Hour after hour feeling unwell and worrying about how the future might pan out. Every day merged into one. My record label had decided to continue releasing music throughout COVID-19, so I spent day after day running a record label from a small village in Sweden. It had a massive impact on many projects but again, it was impossible to measure it against anything else. I just got my head down and worked incredibly hard to try and make things work.

We had our twelve-week scan in Sweden. I was unable to attend. Our child was healthy and things were looking good. We finally announced the news to our wider friendship group and I will always remember the wonderful love and support we received. People seemed to really try to hold on to and celebrate any good news that did come their way.

The UK started to loosen restrictions and it was time for Amanda and I to return to our lives back in London. On 26th May 2020, we boarded a plane to London Stansted. The feeling landing back on UK soil can only be described as eerie. It was as if we were in the movie, '28 Days Later' just without the zombies. We came into contact with more people travelling home from Stansted Airport to South London than we did throughout ten whole weeks in Sweden. The mask wearing general public's behaviour seemed odd. The government and media had no doubt whipped the nation up into a worried frenzy. We were incredibly uncomfortable and just wanted to get back on the plane we had just disembarked from.

As we moved into the summer months, Amanda was able to go back to work in her studio. She attended just four days' work before restrictions were again introduced. These restrictions particularly affected us, as I was not allowed to attend a single pregnancy appointment at the hospital. Amanda would have to attend on her own whilst I sat outside in the car park. Every little bit of news about my child came relayed from Amanda. All pregnancy clubs and activities were cancelled. We met no other parents and had zero classes to prepare us for what was to come. We were having a baby boy.

Caspian was born on 27th October 2020. It was a four-day labour finally requiring an emergency C -section which I attended. The hospital allowed me to stay overnight but I kept my head down and managed to stay for the whole of the following day. I was ordered to leave Amanda and my child at 6pm and was told I could return at 10am the next morning. Without going into detail, Amanda had a horrific evening, even if it didn't show.

We were desperate to get our family home and to start our new lives but there were certain checks that needed to be carried out to make sure Caspian was healthy and happy. This meant that I watched the funeral of my Auntie Mary who had died alone in a care home, via Zoom whilst holding my 13-hour-old baby. It was emotional.

The next phase was without doubt the most challenging period for our now slightly larger family. We could no longer 'sit it out'. Before we could do anything, Christmas 2020 was upon us in a flash and there was another impending lockdown. Could we see our families for Christmas? We were lucky enough to head back to Norfolk to see my family just prior to Christmas. We had a walk around a lake and sat outside in my sister's garden, eating a takeaway. The mood in the camp was mainly frustration by this point.

Every day that passed, rumours of another lockdown became louder. We had booked flights to go to Sweden for Christmas Day. The day before we were due to fly, country after country after country announced that they were banning flights from England. At 7pm, that day, Sweden was added to the list of countries not accepting Brits. At 10pm, I had a phone call letting me know that my mother had been admitted to hospital. We were due to fly at 6am the next day. Should we risk it? Would they let me in? Would I have to wave goodbye to Amanda and Caspian at the gates? What if my mum deteriorated and I couldn't get back?? What if we had to spend another three months in Sweden?

The good news is that my mum was discharged from hospital and we were allowed on the flight. It was eerily quiet and was one of the more pleasant experiences of flying during the pandemic. Upon our arrival, we were welcomed into the country by photographers, journalists, radio presenters and loud music. We were on the final flight which would accept foreigners. We spent three weeks in rural Sweden where we were able to put COVID-19 out of our minds. On Christmas Day, I got down on one knee and asked Amanda to marry me. She said yes! Another positive memory that shines through an otherwise unpredictably dark time.

Upon our return to the UK in January 2021, the country was going into yet another lockdown. We had to make plans and execute some pretty big changes to make things work. We were living in a one -bed apartment and Caspian lived in the corridor of our flat for the first nine months of his life. The first floor flat just didn't suit the needs of a family with a newborn. We had to move home as soon as possible!

Yes, we needed to move home but we were only able to apply for a mortgage from one person's salary. We were extremely lucky that family members stepped in to help us. This allowed us to raise the funds we needed. Buying a house rarely goes to plan and this time was no different. We were completely packed up and ready to move, living out of boxes, when it suddenly became a real possibility that the whole purchase might yet fall through. We held our breath, borrowing yet more money (this time, from my mum) and finally completed the move in September 2021!

At first, I felt incredibly fortunate to be in a job that enabled me to keep working throughout COVID-19. As I had become aware at the beginning f the pandemic, with a phone and a laptop, I could just about tread water. As a record label, we had spent considerable time throughout 2019 building a solid foundation for what was a relatively new business. We had been busy signing artists, recording records and preparing marketing plans for multiple artist campaigns. When COVID-19 hit, we decided to just 'crack on'. We released song after song, watching as the live music business in particular, crumbled. I watched artists' careers disintegrate. I watched great friends lose jobs on a weekly basis. It was tough to watch and I felt a real sense of guilt that we were quietly, and truthfully, unsuccessfully still "going about our business". We were running campaigns at forty per cent because that's all we could do.

It is only now, that as a record label, we are really beginning to suffer from being in second gear for two years. Our long-term investment partner has done the sums and decided it is not worth rolling the dice for 2023. We now have to find a new partner and in the current climate, that won't be easy. There is a very strong chance that by January 2023, I will have to update that CV and start looking for a new job.

I do however have an absolutely wonderful son.

PART II

SNAPSHOTS FROM THE UK

Some contributors chose to write shorter pieces, and these are all from the UK.

New beginnings

The writer moved from Buckinghamshire to live in rural Worcestershire, U.K. With her new partner, they had decided to have a fresh start in the country, finally achieving their dream of living closer to nature and being more self-sufficient. So when the pandemic struck she was not living close to any immediate family or friends.

Not long before the pandemic, I moved from the London area to Worcestershire. Having been through a traumatic marriage break up the year before, at last I was about to live my long-awaited dream of living in the countryside and getting involved in a rural community. I found, however, even though I was living where I had always wanted to live, the pandemic brought many unforeseen problems to someone who was new to the area.

Where do I start to describe what lockdown has been like for me? So many little events and "not so little" events happened, all of which brought a myriad of mixed emotions. The first thing I can remember about when lockdown was announced was wondering, " how will I get through the endless days of nothingness?" Living in rural Worcester was still a new experience, as I had moved away from my usual support circle of family and friends.

The search for supermarket delivery slots was an occupation for sure. I live in a small rural village surrounded by farms and was a relative newcomer, but the local community was all embracing and I was soon part of the local WhatsApp group. This proved invaluable for information and help if needed. Friday was a highlight of the week, watching streamed opera and West End shows, but the most memorable was Andrea Botticelli singing in a deserted cathedral. I think it was in Milan with footage of empty city streets, which was so moving and very chilling, as no one really knew what was to come.

As time passed, routines were established: walking the dog, making bread and tending to my vegetables. My vegetable patch was a great occupation for me, planting the seeds, nurturing the seedlings, planting them out and watching them grow large enough to be harvested. I had not grown any vegetables before so I was very impressed with what my little patch produced: potatoes, runner beans, cauliflower, cabbages, beetroot and carrots, along with tomatoes, cucumbers and peppers in the green house. With these and with the eggs from my hens, I could produce a complete meal. I count myself so lucky to have lived through the various lockdowns surrounded by fields and trees. I had plenty of work to do on my land to keep me from going completely stir crazy. I also took up knitting again, as my first grandchild was on its way. It had been many years since I knitted anything and I found it very therapeutic to rekindle an old hobby.

One of the hardest lockdown experiences was trying to deal with my elderly mum who lived one hundred and fifty miles away, as she was taken from a hospital stay to a care home, where I was not able to visit her. Nine months later she died at the age of ninety-eight and I had not had the opportunity to say goodbye to her. The stress of trying to sell her house to pay for her care and doing it all remotely, with everything taking extra time because of COVID-19, was extremely difficult but I managed to complete the process a month before my mum died.

Several more lockdowns followed and plans to see family were all cancelled which was hard to take, as we had seen virtually nothing of each other since the pandemic began. I didn't get to see my daughter-in- law until a couple of weeks before she had her baby and I needed to see her to make her pregnancy real. I knew of a few deaths from COVID-19 and from the vaccination, but no-one close, so I was not touched that deeply by the pandemic other than the loss of my freedom and the disappointment of holiday cancellations. But these were a small price to pay for keeping safe from the virus.

At the time of writing, (March 2022) the world is still waiting to recover and I wonder if some people in some nations will ever regain the lives they had before the pandemic...I truly pray that they will, as the cost to humanity has been very high in many other ways than just COVID-19.

I survived lockdown...
and I've got fourteen T-shirts to prove it

The writer lives in Norfolk with his partner and his 100-year-old mother and is lucky enough to divide his time between town and country. His hobbies include collecting vinyl, keeping up with new fiction, cycling and playing table tennis. Richard has also written two novels, that he would like to see published before he dies.

Like you, I've had my share of lockdown moments, but don't panic because I'm not about to bore you with my experience of the "Great Awfulness." Mainly, I want to talk about my T-shirt collection.

Yes, you heard right. I've long been a fan of this simple garment. I suspect seven years at school wearing a suit and tie may have had something to do with it. As a consequence, I now have lots of T-shirts, in all colours and designs, most of them well-washed and well-worn. Strange then, that my relationship with this most humble of garments has recently changed.

One day, at the start of lockdown, I happened to mention to a music journalist on Instagram, that I liked his T-shirt design. A few days later, said T-shirt arrived in the post - free, gratis, no charge. OK, it was only a T-shirt, but I was strangely moved by a gift from a stranger. Remember, this was a time when talk was all about the virus from the east. This was when people were avoiding others, rather than reaching out to them.

Next up, I was seduced into buying a black and gold tee bearing the logo 'Warrior of Happiness.' I didn't need another T-shirt and the colours weren't good, but that didn't matter: at a time of misery, I was attracted by a logo that warmed the heart. It seems I had the start of a new collection.

It wasn't long before T- shirts, three and four, dropped in the post. After an ankle fusion, there were periods of discomfort that only swigging from a bottle of morphine relieved. Could that be why I ordered up the Acid House and Club House T shirts, with their sharp designs? Maybe, in some strange way, I wanted a reminder of those long nights of pain.

The early months of COVID-19, proved frustrating as my mum's stay with us turned from temporary to full-term. Mum, at 100 years of age was no problem, but we now understood that only her death would see a return to the freedom we had previously enjoyed. No wonder, Sue and I were desperate for change. I'm guessing such thoughts were behind the Revolution T-shirt.

I expect we all recall that time during lockdown, when every week brought about another restriction, when suddenly, everybody was Zooming friends to exchange box-set ideas, recipes and favourite albums? For me, this kick-started a renewed passion for music, celebrated with a 'Strawberry Fields' tee and a 'Made in Detroit' special. What better way to celebrate the music of the Beatles and Tamla Motown?

This year, for reasons that I've been unable to fathom, problems seemed to have hung around, refusing to leave. We're talking here about health concerns, caring issues and access to grandchildren. To get through the days and weeks, Sue and I have gradually stripped life back to its essentials; down to friends, conversation and tea, ideally, enjoyed, outside in the sunshine. Nothing else seemed to matter much. It would be about this time that I ordered a lovely hippy-dippy tee, featuring an owl and a reminder 'to look for magical moments.' The point being - if you're not looking, you'll miss them.

I should point out that I wasn't buying any old T-shirts: these were Instagram one-offs, so not cheap. Why, then, was I buying them? I suspect it was because I wanted a new wardrobe for when life returned to normal. It took a while to realise I was already living in the new normal.

Now here comes the strange part. Two years on, and I have fourteen brand new T-shirts, all unworn. Presently, they sit in two drawers, neatly folded, waiting for me to be ready.

Well, as of June 2022, I'm still not quite there. With the fall in COVID-19 numbers I got excited, but then Putin started up, then came another ankle fusion and then a family issue introduced a fourth person to the household, ratcheting stress levels up another notch. For the time being, at least, the T-shirts' drawer remains closed.

I hope my tale has connected with you. At the very least, you will have something to look out for. See me in a new top, with a new smile and you'll know things are on the up. I really can't wait.

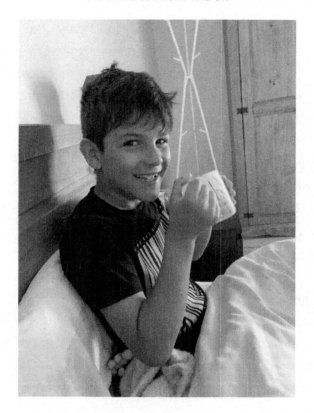

Leo's story
by Leo

Leo is now ten years old, but was eight when lockdown started. He has four younger brothers and two dads. He likes to play on his PlayStation, Switch and mobile phone. He's good at football, athletics and swimming.

In the first lockdown, (March 2020) I heard that schools were shutting. I was quite excited and also happy because then I didn't have to go to school which was boring. Every day I would wake up at 7am. Sometimes I would watch television in my room or sometimes I would play on my games and talk to my friends on my headset. I really loved playing Fortnite, but annoyingly my mum and dad put controls on it. At 9am 'home-school' would begin. I would watch Jo Wicks and do P.E. Sometimes my grandma would join in but that was so embarrassing. Then I would start some work – just English and maths really – which my school sent everyone, online. For history I would watch episodes of 'Horrible Histories', which are twisted stories from the past. I would have a break before lunch and again at lunchtime. In the afternoon, I would go on YouTube and choose a picture to draw. Usually it would be something from Pokémon or Star Wars. Then it was the end of my home-school day and I would watch YouTube on my phone and play on my Play Station again. Usually, I'd also go on the trampoline in our back garden or sometimes in the hot tub.

Although at first when lockdown started, I felt happy, later on it got a bit boring. I could talk to my friends on games or if we FaceTimed, but we couldn't go anywhere. We had to wash our hands for twenty seconds in a special way to make sure we didn't spread COVID-19. My brother got very scared and would never hold hands with anyone. We also couldn't go to shops, but if we went out anywhere we always had to think about 'social distance' (staying two metres apart from other people). That felt weird. I didn't have to wear a mask, though.

When lockdown stopped I went back to school because my mum and dad were key workers. In the summer of July 2020, I went on holiday to France with one of my brothers. We stayed with my grandma and grandpa in their house and spent ages jumping in and out of our little swimming pool and screaming.

In the second lockdown, my brother and I went to school for three days every week, so we didn't have to do home-school. Hurray! But I started my YouTube page, which I've still got and posted some YouTube 'shorts'. At Christmas, we all got COVID-19 and couldn't go to my grandma and grandpa's house for dinner, even though we didn't feel really ill.

Looking back at myself from two years ago, I think I lived through a moment that will be history forever, and might even be an episode on 'Horrible Histories' one day! I don't do Jo Wicks anymore, but I'm good at athletics. I still play my computer games and school's still boring. When all of the lockdowns were over, it felt weird going back to school, but now I'm going into Year 6. I've had my COVD-19 vaccine, but everything's gone back to normal. You don't even stay off school if you test positive and your parents can get a fine from the Government if they take children away on holiday during term time, which is very annoying!

Care Home Story
by SC

SC lives in Norfolk and has a grown-up family. She works for a charity. She tells of adjusting her life in lockdown and the sad story of the experience of her mother dying alone in a care home, an experience which has been replicated across the globe.

So, news was breaking that we might go into lockdown and there were already plans in action to prepare us for working from home. Laptops and mobile phones were issued and I made a space on my dining room table.

We had a couple of weeks' trial run before Boris told us we were to stay at home. Then it became the only option, working from home. I became classed as a keyworker, with a letter to confirm it, if I was ever caught going into the office! I soon moved my workspace to a spare bedroom after finding it too cold and too noisy in my dining room. My husband didn't realise how important it was to be quiet in the kitchen or not to walk in on a Teams meeting. The Internet was not great in that room, and I moved again into our junk room, which was still full of our junk. Health and Safety would not have approved! After twenty-one months of having a make-do space in my house, I finally cleared out the junk room and made it into a proper permanent office. It was a difficult adjustment to start with. I felt isolated and out of touch with what was going on within the organisation and working totally paperless and learning new software via Teams was a challenge. However, I eventually settled into my new work routine. No more time wasted on buses, no expensive car parks, and not as much distraction. The best bit is that I am home straight after the switch off button is pressed. This is my new norm although I do pop into the office once or twice a month, as I prefer it that way.

However, I think my main COVID-19 story is more about my mum. Mum had Alzheimer's with vascular dementia and was living in a care home. Lockdown came for her just before Mothers' Day, no care home visits, so instead I went for a long walk with my daughter and hoped Mum really wouldn't know much about it. She certainly wouldn't have understood any of the COVID-19 situation, but she appeared to be happy in her own world. Next came her birthday in June with still no visits allowed from us. We did manage to get presents delivered and have a Zoom meeting, not great fun with an eighty-six-year-old with dementia, but the carer helped to make it worth it, helping Mum to talk with us, although she did not fully understand how it all worked. But we all laughed, especially Mum. I am not sure of the exact date, but by late summer we (my sister and I) finally got to visit her. This would be outside under a gazebo come rain or shine, a thirty-minute slot with a carer present and a suitable distance between us, with no hugging or contact permitted. Try explaining that to a fit, stubborn eighty-six-year-old with dementia who constantly tried to play musical chairs. Thirty minutes once a week was not a lot but better than nothing. Mum's memory was declining to the point where she sometimes thought we were her sisters, but she always knew we were her family. One day Mum had a fall in the rose bush as she was always trying to pick the flowers. She was taken to hospital to have the branch removed (we thought this was a bad English translation by the carer) but it turned out to be a big piece of the rose bush. We were not allowed to visit and we just got a phone call. At the next visit we could see how this was much more than a rose thorn injury!

Again, I cannot remember the exact date but it was October 2020 and COVID-19 struck the care home, so no visits under the gazebo were allowed until they were clear of it again. Mum was lucky and never tested positive. The home I believe was clear of COVID-19 in late December, but we were still not allowed visits. We dropped Christmas presents off at the door where I didn't see Mum but my sister was lucky enough to see her at the door for a few minutes. One carer stood with her and let my sister talk with her. By this time Boris was talking about allowing one visitor from a family, who must do a lateral flow test at the home and wait for the results, then they could go and see their relative for a thirty minute slot. It had to be same relative the whole time. You could not choose one person one week and then change it the following week. This was such a difficult decision for families to have to make. My sister and I decided this was not fair and our mum would not understand why the other daughter didn't visit. In the event that our mum would die, one daughter would have had regular visits and the other none. How families dealt with this stupid law I really don't know. How did the poor elderly understand it? Did the parent choose, and how did they make that decision without hurting someone? How did broken families agree who could visit? It was a very hard choice to make.

On the 4th February at around 9.30am we got a phone call to say Mum had died in her sleep (it wasn't COVID-19). I was working and my sister got the call. She was told we had thirty minutes to visit Mum before the police coroner took her away. We were too upset to rush over there to do that. It turned out that Mum was found dead at least two hours earlier, so we were not sure why it took them so long to inform us.

It took six weeks to get Mum buried, as the funeral directors were so busy. We were allowed twenty people at the funeral and six at a wake in our house, which were the latest lockdown rules. The vicar kindly told us that we were supposed to socially distance and keep to our own households, but he also said that he had no idea who lived with whom! My son came down from his home in Nottingham, staying the night with us and breaking the rule. There was no way I was going to make him stay in a hotel. We are a family of five, not including my children's partners. My son-in-law was abroad working so we agreed no partners. The wake was then just our family of five. I made a little cream tea, my son had to leave later in the day and get back to Nottingham and my husband had his first COVID-19 vaccination booked, so it was a very short wake. My sister held a separate wake at her house for her family of four. The rest of the funeral party all went to their homes straight after the funeral.

COVID-19 and the government rules robbed my family of the last few precious months of my mum's life as it had been a year of no kisses or hugs and I hadn't seen her for nearly six months before she died. Of course, I know other families who have suffered more.

We had lots of planned events cancelled or put on hold but to finish on a good note, one event did still go ahead which was my husband's godson's wedding. Restrictions in place meant it wasn't the event they had planned. They could only have a few guests at the church, so they invited the closest family members. However, the rest of their original guests turned up, dressed up and all waited behind the small church wall. The photographer took lots of photos of us all and the bridal party talked to us over the church wall after the service. We went to the local pub, six people allowed per table outside so no problem there except for maybe a little table-hopping! The happy couple went back to a family house for a barbeque. They now say it was much more special, than the large expensive wedding they had originally planned.

Time is precious and COVID-19 has made me realise that more than ever. No-one knew how to deal with it correctly with rules and regulations to protect us, which sometimes seemed to lack any common sense. We have all been affected by it, that is one thing for sure.

Family Bubble
by Tracy

Tracy lives in North-West Kent with her husband and three sons. She has worked part-time for a local company for many years. She was furloughed during lockdown, whilst her husband was required to 'work from home.'

I am a mother of three sons, all of whom were in their early twenties at the start of the first lockdown in March 2020. I worried every time they went out to the pub, nightclubs, music gigs, on holidays and even out in their cars. Often there would be phone calls in the middle of the night or the early hours of the morning and I would have to go out on a 'rescue mission', not only for my son but usually for their friends too!

Before we went into lockdown, my eldest son and his girlfriend went to Milan. They arrived at the airport in Italy and were quite shocked when they were met by a man in a white hazmat suit and temperature gun - Italy had already had its first cases of COVID-19. Their temperatures were fine so they were allowed into the country! They visited all the tourist sites and went to a football match without any problems. They arrived at the airport back in England where there weren't any checks - only to find out that the equivalent to a biological bomb had gone off at the football stadium they had attended, infecting thousands of fans. Luckily enough they both escaped the germs and didn't test positive for COVID-19, but my son's company and his girlfriend's school made them isolate for two weeks anyway. Around that time my sister-in-law came to stay with us. My husband said, "You know Jake has just returned from Milan?". He had to repeat this several times because she hadn't been aware of the virus that was beginning to spread around the world and hadn't understood what he was referring to, until he pointed out the news coming from Milan. Even then, she wasn't concerned about catching this 'reported' virus. Luckily, everyone remained healthy, but not long afterwards the Government made an announcement on the television that shops, entertainment venues, restaurants and workplaces would be shutting down. We were shocked, but also quite excited, as we had never experienced this before.

All three sons lived at home, so when lockdown started I knew exactly where they were and did not need to worry any more. It was such a relief to be honest. But there were other changes too.

My husband was told, like many others, to work from home. We turned a room that we hadn't been using into his office so he could work effectively from there, allowing him to pop in and out to join in with our antics. His journey time went from two hours' drive a day to a two-minute walk, but he was quite often still late!

All three girlfriends moved in as lockdown started. So then there were eight of us and a dog called Rusty, who found lockdown very tiring, as everyone wanted to take him on a walk for their daily exercise.

In the autumn of 2019, we'd had a big extension done so that our kitchen, dining area and living room became more or less open plan. As part of this, we extended both our conservatory and patio. We'd had the half wall of our old conservatory rebuilt, so that we now have a massive glass patio door that opens out to the width of the whole conservatory, overlooking the garden and opening out onto a much bigger patio. Luckily, it was all finished by the time lockdown started as it gave us so much more outdoor space.

The weather was lovely right from the start. This allowed us to spend a lot of time in the garden, enjoying the sunshine and making various things. The boys and their other halves made bird nesting boxes, squirrel picnic benches, hot tubs out of wheelie bins and exercise equipment. We would do yoga and exercise in the sun as well.

We would take it in turns to go and queue up at the supermarket to get our provisions and bring them home to the rest of the awaiting group to see what we had managed to purchase. There would be stories to tell of empty shelves (funnily enough we always managed to get beer and gin), of what the outside world was doing and how people were behaving, whilst we all helped to disinfect and dry the shopping before putting it away.

Every weekend instead of going out, we would take it in turns to cook our signature dishes, have bottomless brunches and arrange themed barbecues (Mexican, Greek, Italian etc) so that we wouldn't tire of them, and of course we made plenty of cakes and biscuits, flour permitting.

We spent more time in the evenings together, watching films and box sets, playing games, taking part in weekly quizzes and Bongo's Bingo that appeared online - normally with a drink or two. I did feel sorry for the recycling people when they had to collect the bottles.

I consider myself privileged and very lucky to have been able to spend this time with my family, as they were all extremely good company and a pleasure to be with, and I know so many people were unable to do this.

PART III

PANDEMIC POEMS

One contributor chose poems as his preferred genre, and he wrote many poems during lockdown. He performs these as part of his live repertoire. Here is a selection of them.

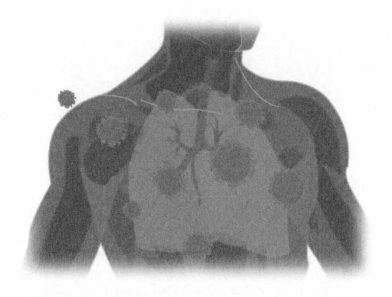

Rob is a Dudley-born comic and singer from North Cornwall. He has performed all over the British Isles and in Australia.

Facebook Thinks I'm Boris Johnson

Facebook thinks I'm Boris Johnson
No, I'm not
What's he blathering on about now?
He forgot

Facial recognition has me down as a privileged blonde
buffoon
Dyed hair
Stooping as he repeats his soundbites and catchphrases.
Thinks he's Churchill.
Does he care?...
(No)

I got tagged as an old Etonian born in America
I'm from the Midlands
He's a famous, over-privileged megalomaniac
Worth millions

There's online confusion that I'm the Prime Minister
I'm more sprightly
Has he ever been to Dudley?
Unlikely

I could be a double for a Bullingdon Club bully
At PMQs
The "World King" waffling at Westminster
What's there to lose?... (apart from my self-respect)

I could avoid answering questions and spout meaningless statistics
In the House
Show off my apparent knowledge of private school-acquired Greek and Latin linguistics
To my spouse...
(to be)

I could stand in front of a big red bus claiming we send £350 million a week to the EU...
And lie
I could blame everything on Europe and get Brexit done
Why?

I didn't pay my taxes?

I didn't pay my taxes?
I didn't pay my dues?
I didn't sleep with hookers
It's really all fake news

I didn't cheat on spouses
I didn't collude with Russians
My son-in-law certainly wasn't involved
In Moscow-based discussions

I didn't dodge the draft five times
I didn't call heroes losers
I had a bone spur in my foot
And some very painful bruises

I didn't call Mexicans rapists
I didn't support white supremacists
Or lie about Obama's birth
(Though he really is my nemesis)

I don't do sexual misconduct
Or grab women where I shouldn't
I never bragged about it, no
I really, really wouldn't

I didn't mock disability
Or try to stop investigations

I didn't appoint my family
To represent this nation

I didn't rig the election
And I won't rig it this time
I'm a very stable genius
And I've never committed a crime

I'm not a playground bully
Or a self-obsessed spoilt brat
I'm a liar who just loves lying
And a nasty, evil twat.

My Bubble

You're my bubble…

You're my globe of soap
You're my ray of hope
You're my Covid liaison
You're my other maison
You're my refuge, asylum
I know your numbers, I dial 'em
You're my walking buddy
We get out, we get muddy
You're my piece of sanity
When my soul's all granite-y
You're my Scrabble nerd
You're my triple word
You're my crossword puzzler
You're my cosy nuzzler
You're my wild rover
You're my quilt puller-over
You're my piece of mind
You're unfailingly kind
You're my get-together
You're my, you know, whatever
Nothings too much trouble
You're my bubble

Cummings Moral Shortcomings

We've all heard the pun about Cummings and goings
But this time the lies are so obviously showing
The PM's puppeteer who prefers "preferential"
On an ego-trip road trip that was never "essential"
We were told not to travel, by car, train or bus
But there's one rule for them and another for us

Those people in my house

In this time of isolation, in this atmosphere of gloom
There are lots of different people that I let into my room
Different members of the family, an old college friend from
Frome
Although some have coughs and sneezes that could send
me to the tomb
We laugh, we have a natter, to relieve the sense of doom
And disperse imaginary thunder clouds that often tend to
loom
And which make my mind regress until I'm back there in
the womb
And then they're gone. They disappear, just like that! Ka-
boom!
As I end my online meeting that I pre-arranged with...
A well-known cloud-based video-conferencing service

Two Metres Apart

Now give me a hug, I'm a super bug
I started out in old Wuhan
My plan is to select, and then infect
Every boy, girl, woman and man
And once I get inside of you
I'll give you something much, much worse than common
flu
But to avoid me there <u>is</u> one thing that you can do
Just keep two metres apart

Chorus:
(You've gotta keep) Two metres apart
That's what the scientists say
Two metres apart
If you really wanna spoil my day
Just keep your distance and wash your hands
If you really wanna piss me off and spoil my plans
Of locating and invading your grandads and your grans
Just keep two metres apart

I am scared of no one, I pick who I choose
I'm a traveller and no mistake
I got into politicians and the Prince of Wales
It really is a piece of cake
And if you have an underlying disease
I'll get into your lungs and your capillaries
But there's one thing you can do, everybody agrees

Just keep two metres apart

Chorus followed by
Two metres apart
Two metres apart
Two – metres – a- paaaaarrrrt

GLOSSARY

A&E – Accident & Emergency

ACAS – Advisory Conciliation & Arbitration Service

BPM – beats per minute

EU – European Union

ICU – Intensive Care Unit

PMQs – Prime Minister's Questions (in the UK Parliament)

PPE – personal protective equipment

NHS – National Health Service

VPN – virtual private network

FCO -Foreign & Commonwealth Office

PCR – a test to detect the COVID-19 virus

PET Scan – used to evaluate presence of disease or infection e.g. cancer

SEND – Special educational needs and disabilities

111 – National Health Service telephone number to get medical advice

Bubbles – (in the context of the COVID-19 pandemic) close personal contacts with people who did not need to wear a mask

Coronaphobia – excessive anxiety about COVID-19

Dominic Cummings – former Chief Adviser to British Prime, Boris Johnson

De rigueur – a custom that is very commonplace

Fogging procedure – usually using a Fogging machine or similar, whereby very fine droplets of disinfectant are sprayed over a relatively large area of a room/shelving/equipment etc

Furlough – employee given temporary leave of absence, to meet the needs of the employer and where the employee is expected to return to work at a later date.

Hazmat – suit worn to protect against hazardous materials

Herd immunity – the percentage of people who need to be immune against a contagious disease

R before 1 – the rate at which the infection rate is falling should be less than one

Rule of Six – UK Government law during the Covid-19 pandemic, which limited the number of people who could meet either indoors or outside, to six people.

WeChat – Chinese messaging app

ABOUT JOANNA O'DONOGHUE

Jo lives and works in Norfolk in the UK. She is a former teacher and currently works as a self-employed education consultant and counsellor.

She has two children and three grandchildren.

Her passions include travelling and reading, and she has always dreamed of writing a book. A compilation of other people's work and an introductory chapter is the first stage of this journey.

Follow Jo on Facebook
@ Jo O'Donoghue. Author
and
on Instagram
@joodonoghueauthor

MORE TESTIMONIALS

This is a powerful collection of writings from around the world, written by those who survived COVID-19 but whose lives were touched by it in ways that are irreversible. It documents the commonalities of experience - initial disbelief, fear, the difficulties of maintaining ordinary domestic life, disruption of travel - which affected people similarly wherever and whoever they were. But then the differences emerge. There are those for whom the quality-of-life changes for the better – "now I had so little responsibility, a time to reflect" - and those who experienced the illness itself, which, pre vaccination was so unaccountably horrible and terrifying. There are also those who found that all the other health issues that have to be faced in normal times- pancreatic cancer, dementia, Crohn's disease, continue in a time of COVID and are made so immeasurably worse by it. There are also those who lost family and friends.

The writers are determined, empathetic, resourceful people, often carers, educationalists, travellers, living life passionately and to the full, but all of them experience the same sense of dislocation and awareness of the utter fragility of the lives we have built, dependent on technology, on our ability to travel, on the assumed abundance of food and medicine. At different times and in different places across the world each of these commonplaces were eroded and challenged, and for some were replaced by a dystopian present of threats and fear and confinement, of political systems that met with repression the desperate challenges of COVID-19 - or were merely inadequate or chaotic in their protection of the most vulnerable.

The skull beneath the skin of our precarious way of life was made clear during COVID: but babies were born, houses bought and sold, new relationships forged. We came through, and if, as one writer said, 'our lives are a little more fragile than we ever realised' maybe that is a good thing. We know now, as the Ukrainians and Afghans do and our grandparents always did, that nothing, not even normality, can be taken for granted.

Mel. Retired teacher/ gardener

Close connection with others is a basic human need. So how do we survive when what sustains us threatens our very existence? Joanna's collection of lockdown experiences fittingly gathered from across the globe offers valuable insight into the myriad of struggles, challenges and triumphs. Sometimes amusing, almost always moving, these individual accounts form a fascinating record that not only gave validation to my own experience, but also will help my toddler grandchildren make sense of theirs in the years to come. Thank you Joanna!

Sue Russell. Life Writer

Printed in Great Britain
by Amazon

13194143R10163